How to Build Treehouses, Huts & Forts

Designs and Illustrations

by

David Stiles

Guilford, Connecticut

An imprint of Globe Pequot

Distributed by NATIONAL BOOK NETWORK

ISBN: 978-1-4930-3673-8

Library of Congress Cataloging-in-Publication data is available on file.

∞™ The paper used in this publication meets the minimum requirements of American National Standard for Information Sciences—Permanence of Paper for Printed Library Materials, ANSI/NISO Z39.48-1992.

Printed in the United States of America

TABLE OF CONTENTS

Introduction

If you have taken shop classes in school you may know enough to make several of these projects, but if you want to learn more, get some books on basic carpentry from the library and study them. Better yet you read our book *Woodworking Simplified - Foolproof Carpentry Projects for Beginners* which teaches you the basics about tools, measuring, sawing, drilling, nailing and how to join pieces of wood together. It is written for adults, but I think you will find it easy to understand. It has a lot of illustrations (like this book) and some simple-to-make projects like a tool box, toy chest, and a workbench, to name a few.

You also might be interested in some of our other books which are:
Treehouses You Can Actually Build
Kid's Furniture You Can Build
Playhouses You Can Build
Rustic Retreats - A Build-It-Yourself Guide
Cabins - A Guide to Building Your Own Retreat
Sheds - A Do-It-Yourself Guide for Backyard Builders

Any of these books can be ordered from our web site:

www.stilesdesigns.com

A Note to Your Parents

As you can probably tell from this book, I think **KIDS ARE GREAT !** Never is there going to be a time in their lives when they are going to be more enthusiastic, have more energy and think more creatively.

You, on the other hand, are wiser and have the benefit of experience that you can pass on to your child. At times you may have to temper your child's enthusiasm to rush outside and begin building a huge project with a reality check. Kids don't realize you have to plan, buy materials, bring them home and assemble the tools that will be needed. If you can do this together, they will know what to expect the next time you build something.

You need patience - a lot of patience, to build something with a kid, because they are so excited about getting the project completed in order to play in it. Resist the temptation of taking over when you see your child is having difficulty driving a nail straight or sawing a straight line. Show them how to do it right, or if the job is too difficult like sawing a board lengthwise, give your child another job like sanding, to keep them occupied while you do the job yourself.

If you get carried away (as I sometimes do), and get totally involved with a project that you are building with your kid, remind yourself, "It's OK". You are entitled to have fun building something. The project is good therapy for you even if your kid might not appreciate it as much as you would like. Every parent I have talked to who has built a treehouse for their kid has been **IMMENSELY PROUD** of their accomplishment, and some even forget that it was for their kid and not for themselves.

A Word for the Kids

Try to encourage your parents to build stuff with you but **WITHOUT NAGGING THEM.** Try and understand that some of the materials might cost money and offer to pay for some of it out of your allowance. Make plans on paper and show it to them so they can see how sincere you are. Try not to suggest projects that are beyond their capabilities since not everybody is a born carpenter. Try not to laugh if your Dad hits his thumb with a hammer - he is probably darn good at his regular job.

So go easy on Mom and Dad - It's not easy being a parent.

Carpentry Tips

Most of the projects in this book are easy to build. All of them require some knowledge of carpentry, tools and materials. The next few pages contain some basic information that you should know before starting any of these projects.

Lumber

If you are going to buy lumber at a lumber yard or home building supply center, you must be aware that a piece of lumber sold as a 2x4 does not actually measure 2" x 4". Instead, it measures $1\frac{1}{2}$" x $3\frac{1}{2}$". This is because the final size has to be cut (dressed) down to a uniform thickness. (Also, it is easier to say "two by four," than it is to say "oneandonehalfbythreeandonehalf").

To help you understand this better, study the illustration below:

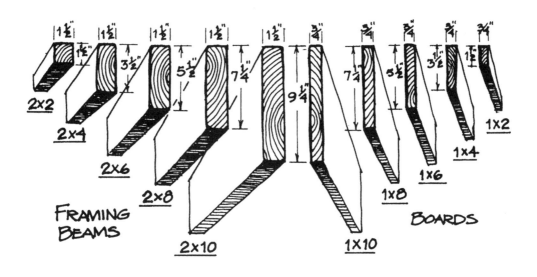

Your Dad already knows that a 2x4 measures $1\frac{1}{2}$" x $3\frac{1}{2}$", but does he know what a 2x8 measures? I bet he thinks it is $1\frac{1}{2}$" x $7\frac{1}{2}$". Test him. (It is $1\frac{1}{2}$" x $7\frac{1}{4}$).

*Note: Dimensions of *underline*pressure treated wood*underline* may vary.

Lumber -continued

Also, check the actual thickness of plywood with a tape measurer before buying it. Sometimes a sheet of plywood sold as 3/4 thick is actually slightly less! (Very sneaky of them)

Lumber is generally sold in two foot increments by the running foot and not the old way using "board feet" which is more difficult to figure out. Don't ask them to cut you a piece less than six feet long because they may not be able to sell you the left over piece and that makes them loose money.

TIP: If your local lumber company delivers lumber free, have them deliver 10% more than you need. Sort through the lumber and have them pick up the bad pieces and take them back. (However, you may be charged 15% more for the returned lumber)

Avoid lumber that has loose knots, especially on the underside of the beam' which could be very weak. Hard knots within the beam are OK.

HARD KNOT OK.

LOOSE KNOT

It is always best to pick out your own lumber at the lumber yard and bring it home yourself.

Inspect each piece carefully to make sure it is nice and straight.

nailing

Here are some helpful hints on how to use a hammer:

To improve accuracy, hold the hammer close to the hammer head when starting to nail.

Once the nail is started, hold the hammer back on the handle to get more power in your stroke.

NOTE:
Look before you nail. Make sure you are not nailing into any knots, (in either piece of wood). Knots are almost impossible to nail into.

If the nail starts to go in crooked, remove it by placing a piece of wood under the hammer head before pulling the nail out. Start again in a different place.

drilling

You should be at least eight years old before attempting to use an electric drill. The reason: There is a lot of torque (turning force) in an electric drill that may spin you around like a windmill. Let Dad or an older brother drill the holes.

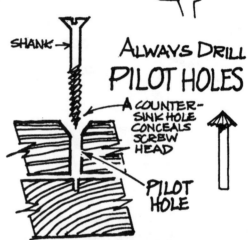

CHUCK
SPEED
REVERSE
TRIGGER

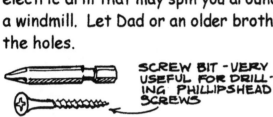

SCREW BIT - VERY USEFUL FOR DRILLING PHILLIPSHEAD SCREWS

TWIST DRILL: CAN BE USED FOR BOTH WOOD AND METAL

SPADE DRILL: FOR DRILLING LARGER HOLES

FLAT

AUGER DRILL BIT - BEST FOR DRILLING INTO TREES AND HEAVY TIMBERS

SHANK →

ALWAYS DRILL PILOT HOLES

A COUNTER-SINK HOLE CONCEALS SCREW HEAD

PILOT HOLE

THE PILOT HOLE SHOULD BE THE SAME SIZE AS THE SHANK OF THE SCREW

TIPS:
Always clamp the wood you are drilling to keep it from turning.
Use screws instead of nails. They hold better and are easier to remove in case you make a mistake!
Keep your body weight directly over the drill and your eye on the bit.

Nails & Screws

Nails come in different sizes and shapes depending upon their intended use. The most common one that you are probably familiar with is, appropriately named, "*Common Nail*". It looks like this   and has a big head.

Since most projects in this book are used outdoors, only buy nails that have a "*galvanized*", light gray coating that keeps them from rusting. DON'T USE OLD SALVAGED NAILS that your grandfather kept in an old coffee can. They are probably rusty, bent, and hard to hammer. Invest some of your allowance in new nails since they are relatively cheap.

Nails are still sold in some places using the outdated symbol "d" which is pronounced "penny" for some unexplainable reason. Ignore this and buy your nails "by the size". A good size to start with is 3" (galvanized) nails used by framers to nail structural beams together and 2" common nails for attaching 3/4" thick siding boards or floor boards (including plywood). For smaller items, such as 1/2" thick trim boards and cabinets, use 1 1/2" finishing nails.

Don't use nails to join heavy beams to trees or large posts. Instead, use 1/2" diameter LAG SCREWS (incorrectly referred to by many people as lag BOLTS).

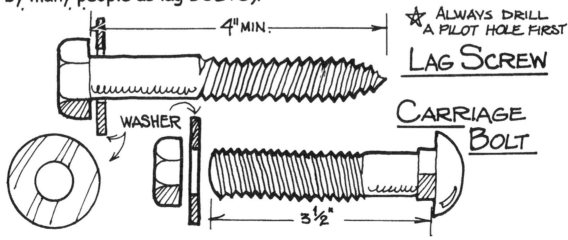

☆ ALWAYS DRILL A PILOT HOLE FIRST

LAG SCREW

CARRIAGE BOLT

4" MIN.

WASHER

3½"

HOW TO INSTALL
LAG SCREWS

• Use lag screws that are at least 1/2" in diameter.

• Thinner lag screws can break off under stress.

• Drill a 1/2" diameter hole near the end of the beam for the lag screw.

• Place the beam against the tree and mark (through the hole) where the screw should go.

• Remove the beam and drill a ⅜" diameter pilot hole where the mark is.

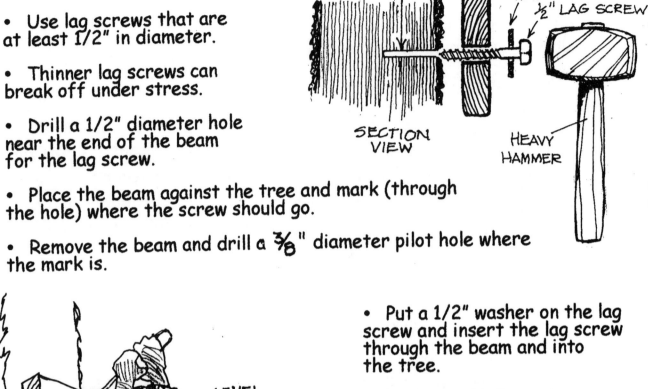

⅜" DIA. PILOT HOLE

BEAM

WASHER

½" LAG SCREW

SECTION VIEW

HEAVY HAMMER

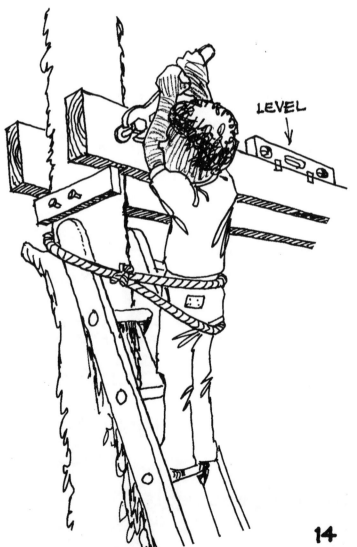

LEVEL

• Put a 1/2" washer on the lag screw and insert the lag screw through the beam and into the tree.

• Hammer the lag screw into the hole in the tree with several hard blows.

• Using a wrench, turn the lag screw one-quarter turn only. Pound the head of the screw very hard and make another quarter turn.

• Do this about six more times to make sure the screw threads are securely caught in the wood fibers of the tree.

• Continue screwing until the washer depresses into the tree.

14

Unlike modern-day builders who
standardize everything into 2 foot
modules, nature builds trees as differently as possible
from one tree to the next. Therefore, it is impossible to
explain exactly how to build anything in a tree since there
are so many variables. The following pages may give you
some general guidelines to help you get started.

TreeHouseTips

LOOK FOR A MONTHLY TREEHOUSE TIP
ON OUR WEB SITE WWW·STILESDESIGNS·COM

One way to provide for movement in the tree is to bolt a steel slide bracket to the tree for the beam to rest on.

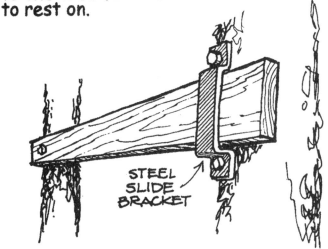

STEEL
SLIDE
BRACKET

Another way to allow for movement is to use 5/8" nylon rope lashings.

↓

Tree Injury

No one wants to hurt a tree, but putting a nail into a tree is like us getting a mosquito bite. Trees are much more likely to die from insects, disease, windfalls or lack of water.

Here is what an expert says: "The wood surrounding the hardware (lag screw) will discolor, but if it is sound to begin with, it will seldom decay to any extent."

From *Tree Maintenance* by P.P. Pirone

Tree Steps

Steps like these can be used provided that they can be attached securely.

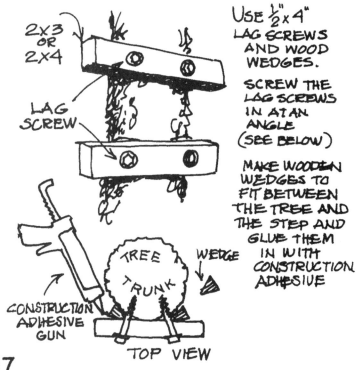

2X3
OR
2X4

LAG
SCREW

USE ½"X4" LAG SCREWS AND WOOD WEDGES.

SCREW THE LAG SCREWS IN AT AN ANGLE (SEE BELOW)

MAKE WOODEN WEDGES TO FIT BETWEEN THE TREE AND THE STEP AND GLUE THEM IN WITH CONSTRUCTION ADHESIVE

CONSTRUCTION ADHESIVE GUN

TREE TRUNK

WEDGE

TOP VIEW

17

TreeHouseTips

Finding the Right Tree

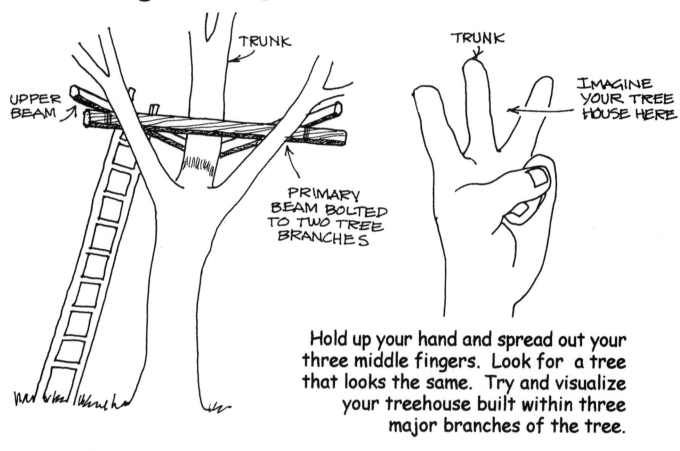

UPPER BEAM

TRUNK

PRIMARY BEAM BOLTED TO TWO TREE BRANCHES

TRUNK

IMAGINE YOUR TREE HOUSE HERE

Hold up your hand and spread out your three middle fingers. Look for a tree that looks the same. Try and visualize your treehouse built within three major branches of the tree.

Using a tall ladder to stand on, attach a strong beam across two branches with 1/2" diameter lag screws. Use this beam as a support for two upper beams. Attach the back ends of the upper beams to the tree and bolt the front ends to the lower beam. Note that the two upper beams can extend (cantilever) past the lower beam to make your treehouse bigger.

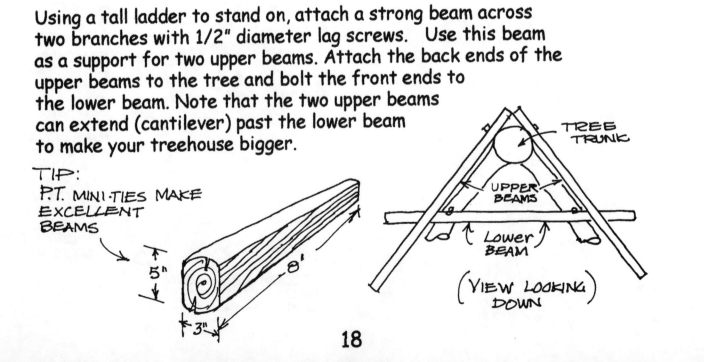

TIP:
P.T. MINI-TIES MAKE EXCELLENT BEAMS

5"

8'

3"

TREE TRUNK

UPPER BEAMS

Lower BEAM

(VIEW LOOKING DOWN)

Platform (floor) Framing

To get the first support beam up into the tree, you may
need to suspend it by rope, higher up into the tree.
Hold the beam temporarily in place with rope
or duct tape and check to make sure
it is perfectly level. You should
be able to find a level in your dad
or mom's tool box. Hold it on top
of the beam and tilt the beam
until the bubble in the glass
vial is dead center. Then drill
a 1/2" diameter *pilot* hole, using
a brace & bit or a battery operated
drill with an auger bit.

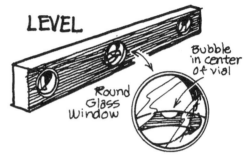

LEVEL

Bubble
in center
of vial

Round
Glass
Window

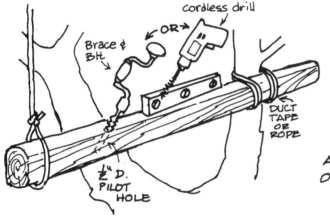

cordless drill

Brace &
Bit

OR

DUCT
TAPE
OR
ROPE

½" D.
PILOT
HOLE

TIP:

AN AUGER DRILL
BIT LIKE THIS →
IS MUCH EASIER
TO USE THAN
ANY OTHER TYPE
OF DRILL BITS

AUGER
BIT →

ATTACH THE BEAM TO THE TREE
WITH ½" OR ⅝" DIAMETER
LAG SCREWS.

(ANYTHING SMALLER WILL
BREAK OFF IN TIME.)

SUPPORT
BLOCK
CUT FROM
2×4

SCREW

PILOT
HOLE

To reinforce the connection
between the branch and the
beam, you can cut a support
block and a wedge using an
electric jig saw. Hold them
in place with construction
adhesive and 5" galvanized
deck screws.

How to Prevent the Wind From Blowing Your Tree House Down

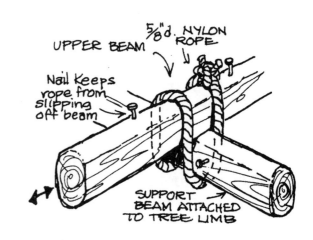

To allow for movement in the branches when the wind blows, attach the beams together with nylon rope. The upper beam should ride freely on top of the lower support beam. This allows the treehouse to be attached to the upper beams and to be independent of the movement of the branches in a wind storm.

NOTE: LARGE BRANCHES CLOSE TO THE GROUND MOVE VERY LITTLE, HOWEVER, BRANCHES HIGH UP IN A TREE CAN SWAY 4" TO 6" IN EITHER DIRECTION.

A FLEXIBLE JOINT SUCH AS THIS CAN SUPPORT A BEAM.

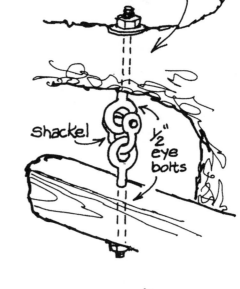

shackel   ½" eye bolts

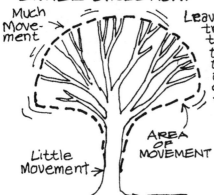

Much Movement

Leaves on the trees resist the force of the wind similar to the sail on a sailboat and cause the tree to bend.

AREA OF MOVEMENT

Little Movement

Ways to prevent a "Blow Down"

1. BUILD CLOSE TO THE GROUND.

2. USE JUST THE TRUNK OF THE TREE TO SUPPORT THE TREEHOUSE WITH DIAGONAL BRACES.

3. "FLOAT" THE PLATFORM FLOOR OF YOUR TREEHOUSE SO THAT IT IS INDEPENDENT FROM THE MOVEMENT OF THE BRANCHES.

... OR YOU CAN ASSUME SOME REPAIRS WILL HAVE TO BE MADE OVER THE YEARS AND NOT WORRY ABOUT IT.

FLOOR FRAMING

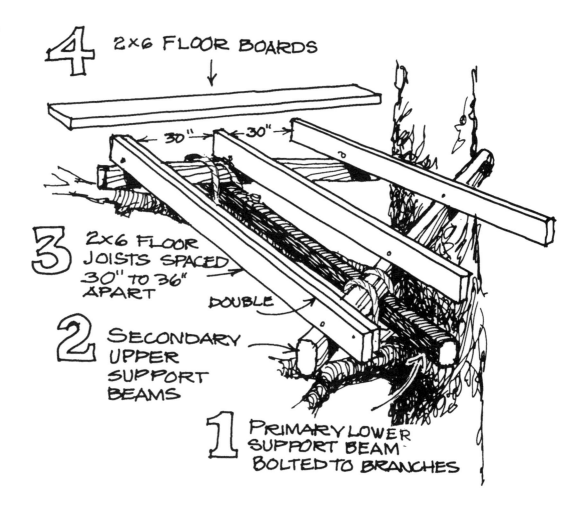

4 2x6 FLOOR BOARDS

30" 30"

3 2x6 FLOOR JOISTS SPACED 30" TO 36" APART

DOUBLE

2 SECONDARY UPPER SUPPORT BEAMS

1 PRIMARY LOWER SUPPORT BEAM BOLTED TO BRANCHES

In this method of framing the secondary beams ride on top of the primary beam allowing for movement in the branches when the wind blows. To keep the secondary beams from sliding completely off the beam underneath in a violent wind storm, attach a rope around the two beams so they can move - but stay in place. The object is to make the treehouse platform independent of the branches supporting it. This precaution is necessary for treehouses built high in the trees where there is more movement in the branches. It is not necessary for treehouses built close to the ground where there is little or no movement in the supports.

SPANS

How far can a beam or board safely span over two supports??? It depends on the thickness or the size of the lumber and how it is laid on the supports.

For instance:

A 1x4 can span 16" laid flat (when used as floor boards).

1x6 can span 18" laid flat (when used as floor boards).

2x4 can span 24" laid flat or 42" if laid on edge.

2x6 can span 36" laid flat or 6 ft. if laid on edge.

2x8 can span 48" laid flat or 8 ft. if laid on edge.

2x10 can span 6 ft. laid flat or 10 ft. if laid on edge.

TIP

If you use scaffolding boards instead of 1" thick floor boards, you can span much greater distances (as much as 8 ft.) and eliminate the need for floor joists.

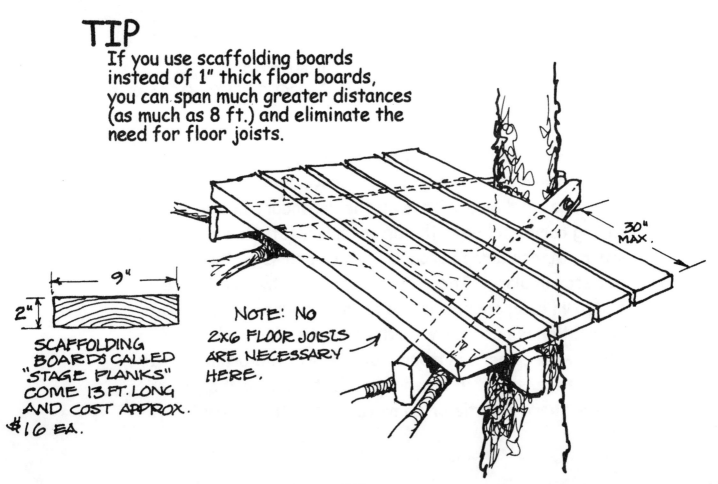

SCAFFOLDING BOARDS CALLED "STAGE PLANKS" COME 13 FT. LONG AND COST APPROX. $16 EA.

NOTE: NO 2x6 FLOOR JOISTS ARE NECESSARY HERE.

22

Easy-to-Build Treehouse

This treehouse can be built in just one weekend (with a little advance work). It was designed to require as little cutting as possible by using four full size sheets of plywood, just as they come from the lumber yard, and one sheet of plywood that has to be cut up into six pieces to form the front and rear walls.

MATERIALS

(1) 6x6 pressure treated post
(1) 80 lb bag sacrete - post base

(3) 2x8 beams 12'-14' long - support beams
(8) 2x4s 8' long - platform frame
(2) sheets 3/4" 4'x8' plywood - floor
(3) sheets 3/4" 4'x8' plywood - roof and walls
(6) 2x4s 8' long- wall framing
(1) 4x4 14' long - railing posts
(2) 2x6 8' long - railing
(6) 1/2" x 4" lag screws & washers
(1) 10 ft. 3/4" dacron rope- tie downs
1 lb 2 1/2" galvanized deck screws
3 lbs. 6d 2" galvanized common nails

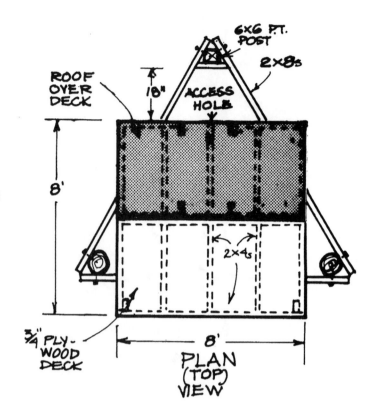

ROOF OVER DECK

6X6 P.T. POST

2×8s

18"

ACCESS HOLE

8'

2×4s

3/4" PLY. WOOD DECK

8'

PLAN (TOP) VIEW

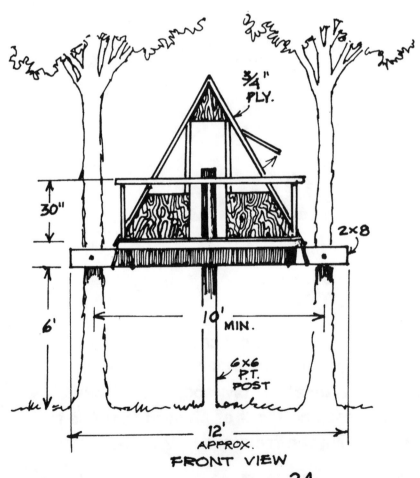

3/4" PLY.

30"

2×8

6'

10' MIN.

6X6 P.T. POST

12' APPROX.

FRONT VIEW

24

This treehouse needs only two trees 10 to 14 feet apart. The third leg of the treehouse is a 6x6 post that is sunk in place before you begin building. The length of the post depends on how high you want the treehouse to be, but you should allow at least 30" to be buried in the ground. Order all the lumber from your local lumber yard and have them deliver it to your home. Most likely you will have to carry all the lumber to your back yard which will require strong arms and gloves.

WHEW !

Post - 6x6 pressure treated or any 7" diameter dead tree that you can find in the woods. Make sure the tree is not rotten by removing the bark and inspecting the wood.

Position the post so that it is the same distance from the other two trees and an equal distance apart.

Use a post hole digger or a small spade to make a 6" diameter hole in the ground. If the ground is really hard, you may need an iron pick to loosen the soil and rocks.

Bring some friends along to help, because this may be hard work especially if the ground is hard.

Once the hole is dug, put a large rock in the bottom of the hole for the post to sit on.

Tilt the post into the hole and bring it upright. Use 2x4s from your lumber pile as braces to temporarily hold the post in place.

BOARD ACTS AS A SHIELD TO KEEP DIRT FROM FALLING IN HOLE.

SACR

25

Set the post in concrete so you won't have to worry when the next hurricane comes. This is easily done by pouring dry Sacrete (about 4" at a time) into the hole and mixing it with a little water while it is in the hole. Use a thin stick to mix the concrete and water by jabbing up and down (called "jitterbugging") in the hole. Don't use too much water as the stiffer the mix, the stronger the concrete will be. Continue filling the hole, 4" at a time, until you reach the top. Make a rounded surface at the top so no rain water will collect there. Let the concrete cure for 24 hours.

(See page 42)

IMPORTANT:

While backfilling the hole, keep checking all the time to make sure the post is plumb (vertical) on all sides.

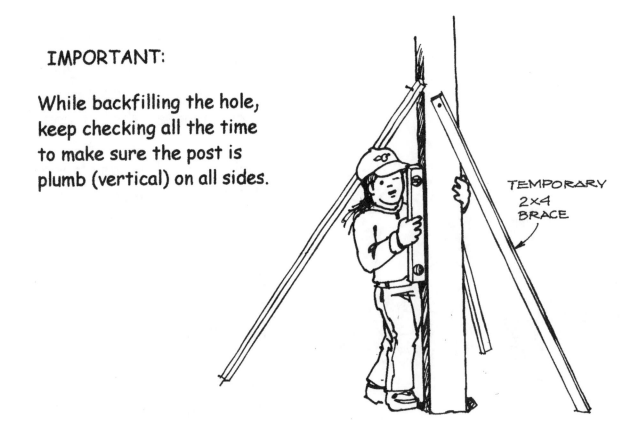

TEMPORARY 2x4 BRACE

SUPPORT BEAMS
STEP 1.

Hold one end of a 2x8 beam up against one of the trees and mark in the center of the beam where the lag screw should go. Allow 5 " to 6" of the end of the beam to extend beyond the tree. Drill a 1/2" diameter hole through the beam. Hold the beam against the tree and make a mark through the hole into the center of the tree. Remove the beam and drill a 3/8" diameter pilot hole 2" into the tree.

Using a socket wrench, screw a 4" long 1/2" diameter lag bolt (and washer) through the beam and into the tree.

STEP 2.

Next swing the other end of the beam up. Make sure it is level and hold it in place with 2x4 props while you repeat step one.
Repeat the same steps with the other two beams making sure that they are all level.

2×8 BEAM

$\frac{3}{8}$" DIA. PILOT HOLE

SOCKET WRENCH

PLATFORM

The platform can be built safely on the ground and hoisted up onto the support beams with the help of a few more hands. You will need seven 2x4s eight feet long and two full size 4x8 sheets of 3/4" thick plywood. (Note: Use exterior grade plywood if you expect the tree house to last more than a few years.)

Begin by cutting 3" off five of the 2x4s and place them side by side, 24" on center, on the ground. These will be your floor joists. Nail an 8 ft, 2x4 to the ends of the joists as shown here.

Check for square by measuring the two cross diagonals- they should be the same.

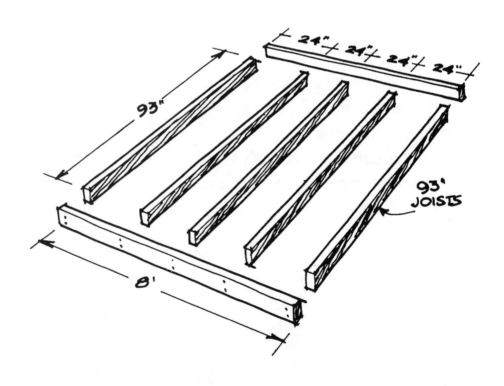

Hoist or push the platform frame up onto the support beams.
Position it so there is about an 18" clearance between the rear
post and the frame. This way there will be room to climb up and
access the treehouse.

To keep the 2x4 in place and allow for some movement in the trees, bore two 3/4" diameter holes in the 2x4's where they lie on the support beams and tie the frame to the support beams using 5/8" nylon rope.

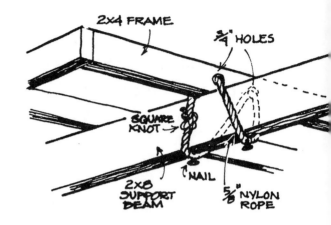

Push two pieces of plywood up onto the platform and nail them down onto the 2x4 frame using 6d (penny) galvanized 2" nails.

HOUSE
Make the roof by pulling two 4'x8' full- size sheets of plywood up onto the platform. Lay them down across from one another so that the ends of the plywood overhang the sides of the platform by one inch. (see sketch)

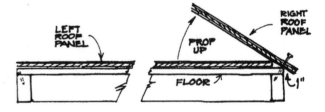

Nail three 10d (3") nails at an angle into the plywood and into the 2x4 frame below. Do the same on the other side, however, to do this you will have to raise the second plywood roof panel with a piece of scrap lumber as a prop in order to get the roof panel to touch the floor of the platform while you put in the three nails. The nails will bend and act as a hinge to keep the roof panels from sliding down off the platform while you nail them to the edge of the platform.

To keep the panels from slipping at the top, screw temporary braces across the two panels at the edges. (Check to make sure that the screws go into the very center of the plywood edge.)

Use these temporary braces to support a scaffolding board which you will need to stand on while you attach the two roof pieces at the top.

To attach the top, use an electric drill with a Phillips head screw bit to screw 2 1/2" galvanized screws, 5" apart, across the top on both sides. Be careful that the points of both screws don't stick out the other side where they could hurt somebody.

FRONT AND REAR WALLS
Framing
Bevel cut two pieces of 2x4 so that they fit between the two roof panels at the bottom. Position the 2x4s so that they are 2 1/2" recessed back from the front edges of the roof. Cut four pieces of 2x4 for the sides of the doorway approximately 5 feet long, and nail them vertically, an equal distant from the center, and 21" apart. Cut two 2ft. pieces of 2x4 for the top and bevel the ends so that they fit between the two roofs and sit on top of the doorway posts. Nail them all together. Cut four more 2x4's, 24" long, to fit horizontally between the doorway and the roof panels, 24" up from the base.

Cut the fifth piece of 3/4" plywood down the middle into two 24" x 96" pieces. Mark and cut the four bottom pieces as shown on the cutting plan. Nail the panels in place, using 2" nails.

31

The top triangle should measure 24"x24"x24", but to play it safe hold the remaining scrap plywood panels in place and mark with a pencil, and cut out the exact triangular shape. Screw the bottom of the triangle to the 2x4 at the top of the doorway and screw through the roof into the top sides of the triangle.

RAILING

Make the railing waist high. (Your waist, not Mom or Dad's). Use 4x4 posts at the corners. Using an electric jig saw cut 3 1/2" x 3 1/2" pocket holes in the plywood for the bottom of the 4x4 posts to slip into. Screw them into place from two sides.

Cut rails from 2x6 lumber and screw them to the tops of the posts by cutting the ends at 45 degrees where they meet at the corners.

If your little brother or sister is going to use the treehouse, it is a good idea to lace some rope from post to post to prevent them from falling off.

LADDER

With the leftover plywood you can cut steps that you can screw to the rear 6x6 post. Make sure the steps are about 10" apart and sand off the edges so that they are smooth to the touch.

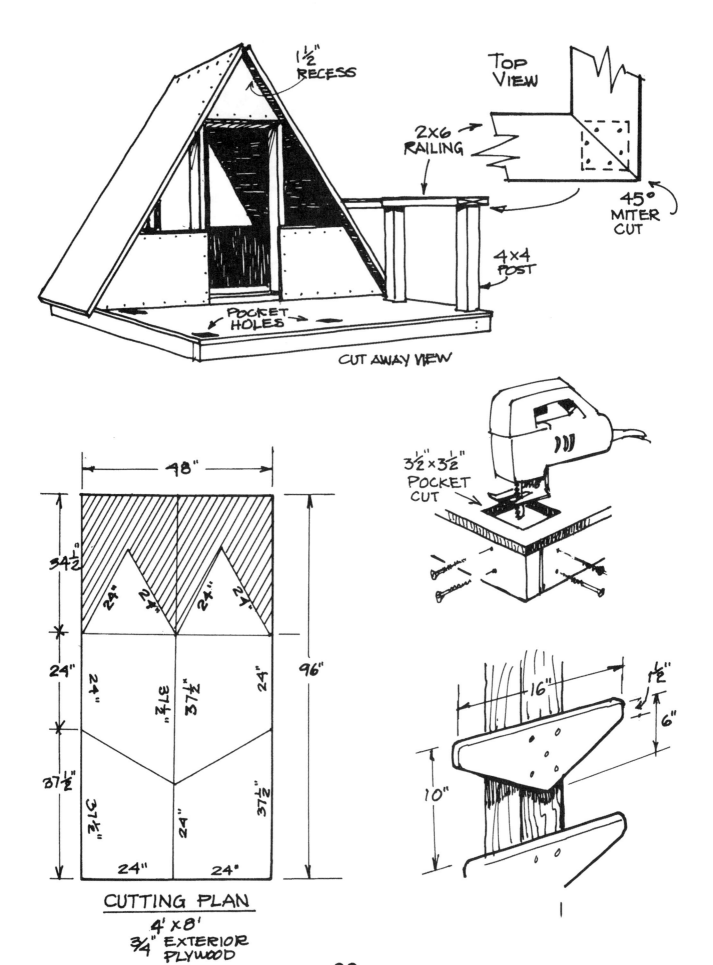

1½" RECESS

TOP VIEW

2X6 RAILING

45° MITER CUT

4X4 POST

POCKET HOLES

CUT AWAY VIEW

3½" × 3½" POCKET CUT

48"

34½"

24"

24"

24"

24"

96"

24"

24"

37½"

37½"

24"

37½"

37½"

24"

24"

24"

24"

CUTTING PLAN

4' X 8'
¾" EXTERIOR PLYWOOD

16"

1½"

6"

10"

33

TreeHut

A treehouse
depends largely
on the types of trees
available. This tree hut is
built on one tree that has at
least two branches and the
trunk to support the corners
of the treehouse. The other
corner is supported by building
a brace up from the trunk.

Since every tree is different,
it is difficult to design the treehouse first and then find a tree
to fit it. It is better to find the
tree first and let it suggest the
shape of the house.

Tree Hut

You can build your tree hut any size you want depending on the size and shape of the tree and the materials you have available, however, if you are the type of person who likes to work from plans, the next few pages are for you. The plans show how a small 5' by 6' tree hut can be built. Feel free to alter them in any way to fit your particular situation and to express your own creative ideas. There are no two tree houses alike (which is how it should be).

One thing all treehouses have in common is a sturdy platform on which the hut sits. Installing the platform can sometimes be the hardest part of the job. Before you begin, look over some of the preceding pages for tips on how to build a level platform in a tree.

One method is to build the platform on the ground and hoist it up into the tree, using a block and tackle. To accomplish this, you will need to do some advance planning and take careful measurements in the tree where the platform will go. Once it is up in the tree, you can add diagonal braces for additional support.

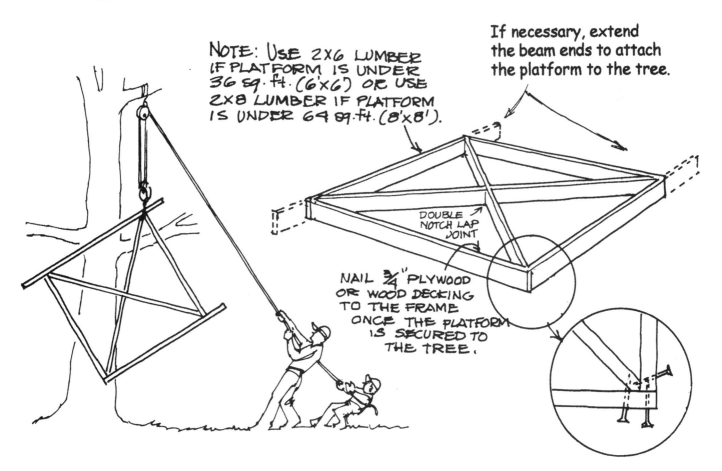

NOTE: USE 2X6 LUMBER IF PLATFORM IS UNDER 36 SQ. FT. (6'X6') OR USE 2X8 LUMBER IF PLATFORM IS UNDER 64 SQ. FT. (8'X8').

If necessary, extend the beam ends to attach the platform to the tree.

DOUBLE NOTCH LAP JOINT

NAIL 3/4" PLYWOOD OR WOOD DECKING TO THE FRAME ONCE THE PLATFORM IS SECURED TO THE TREE.

Hut Framing — Using 2×3 Lumber

THIS DESIGN PROVIDES A MINIMAL AMOUNT OF CUTTING AND A MINIMAL AMOUNT OF WASTE MATERIAL.

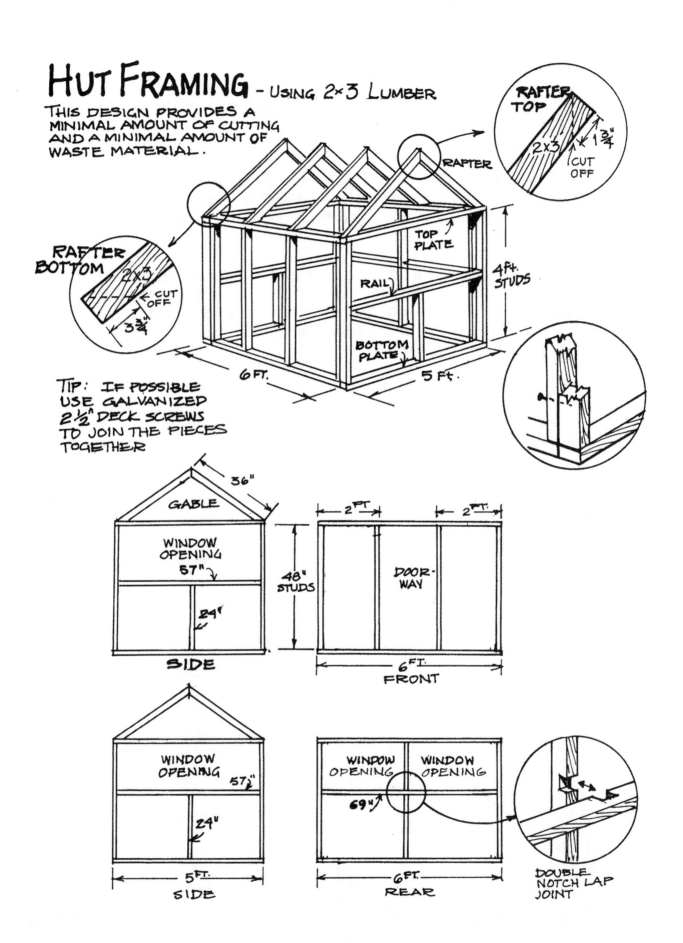

RAFTER TOP

2×3

1 3/4"

CUT OFF

RAFTER

TOP PLATE

RAIL

4 ft. STUDS

BOTTOM PLATE

RAFTER BOTTOM

2×3

CUT OFF

3 3/4"

6 FT.

5 Ft.

TIP: IF POSSIBLE USE GALVANIZED 2 1/2" DECK SCREWS TO JOIN THE PIECES TOGETHER

36"

GABLE

WINDOW OPENING

57"

24"

SIDE

48" STUDS

2 FT.

2 FT.

DOOR-WAY

6 FT. FRONT

WINDOW OPENING

57"

24"

5 FT. SIDE

WINDOW OPENING

WINDOW OPENING

69"

6 FT. REAR

DOUBLE NOTCH LAP JOINT

Hut Siding & Roofing
Siding

Nail 1x6 shiplap siding onto the frame, using 2 1/2" galvanized nails. *(This part is fun and goes quickly)*

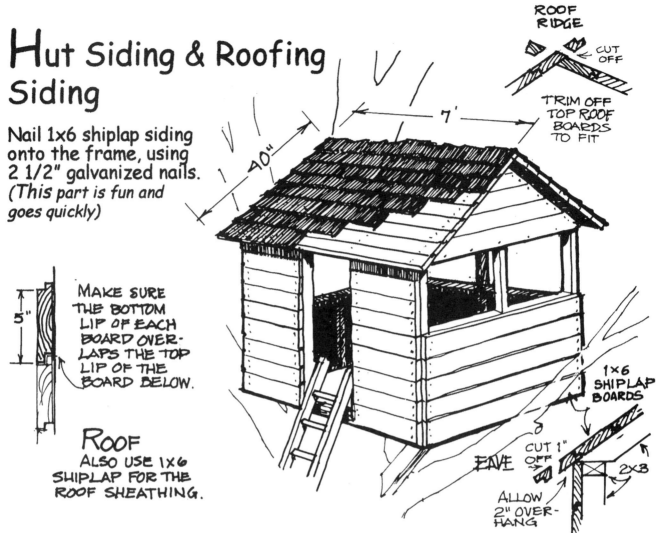

ROOF RIDGE

CUT OFF

TRIM OFF TOP ROOF BOARDS TO FIT

7'

40"

5"

MAKE SURE THE BOTTOM LIP OF EACH BOARD OVER-LAPS THE TOP LIP OF THE BOARD BELOW.

ROOF
ALSO USE 1x6 SHIPLAP FOR THE ROOF SHEATHING.

1×6 SHIPLAP BOARDS

EAVE

CUT 1" OFF

ALLOW 2" OVER-HANG

2×3

Roofing

To make the roof waterproof you can use tar paper, rolled roofing. asphalt shingles (as shown here) or cedar wood shingles.

Instructions for applying shingles are found on the package that they come in.

Remember to start the shingles at the bottom of the roof- not the top.

Each bundle of asphalt 3 tab shingles covers 33 sq.ft.

Materials

Framing - 2x3s

(2) 6'	(2) 5'	Bottom plates
(11)4'	(2) 2'	Studs
(2) 6'	(2) 5'	Top plates
(2) 57"	(1) 64"	Rails
(8) 3'		Rafters

Siding - 1x6 shiplap boards

(20)	2'	Front
(10)	5'	Two sides
(2)	14'	Gables (cut to size)
(5)	6'	Rear

Roof - 1x6 shiplap boards

(16) 7' (Allow 6" overhang each end)
2 bundles, 3-tab asphalt shingles
1 lb. 1 1/4" roofing nails
2 lbs. 2 1/2" (8d) common galv. nails
2 lbs. 2 1/2" galv. deck screws

Secret Escape Hatch

A secret escape hatch is always a good thing to have in case you need to beat a hasty retreat. If you plan ahead, you can make it so no one will be able to recognize it from the ground below.

Before you nail the floor boards down, lay them over the floor framing (joists) and mark the center line of the joists across the floor boards. Cut the floor boards so that they, and the hatch boards, share the same joist support underneath, thus creating a 3/4" lip for the hatch to rest on.

If this is as difficult for you to understand, as it is for me to explain, try figuring it out from this drawing.

Nail two 1x3 boards across the top of the hatch boards to keep them together. Make sure they line up with the other floor boards so that they will be indistinguishable from the rest.

To use the hatch, remove the hatch cover and climb down a rope ladder that you have previously bolted to the floor of the tree house.

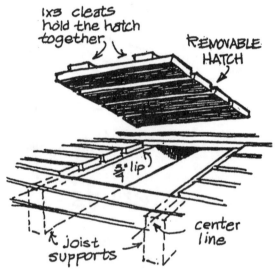

1x3 cleats hold the hatch together

REMOVABLE HATCH

3/4" lip

center line

joist supports

Make your escape hatch the width of YOUR shoulders.

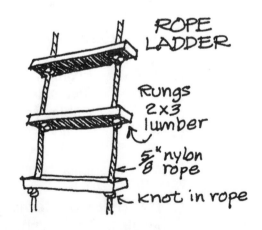

ROPE LADDER

Rungs 2x3 lumber

5/8" nylon rope

knot in rope

Imagine yourself lost in the wilderness with nothing but a hammer and a saw. How would you build a shelter to protect yourself from the wind, rain and wild animals?

The next few pages show you how to build a treehouse from materials found in the woods - well, almost - we've cheated a little and added lag screws and some rope for added strength.

The logs for this treehouse may require some scouting around on your part. Look for four straight trees, approximately 6" to 7" in diameter at the butt (bottom) ends and 12' tall, for the four main posts. Look for fallen trees in the woods that are dead, but NOT ROTTEN, or you may check out vacant building lots that have just been cleared for construction. Ask permission first. If you know someone who owns wooded property you might point out that it is good for the overall health of the woods to thin out the trees so that the healthiest trees have more sunlight. Look for straight trees that are close to the road so they can be transported on top of a car.

Another alternative is old telephone poles which you might be able to buy from your local utility company. Use the thinner, top end which will be lighter and easier to install.

The best type of wood to use for the four main posts is white pine, because it peels easily and is lightweight and easy to carve. If the logs are freshly cut, peel them in the spring when the sap is running and the bark is not firmly attached to the tree. Make 2" wide cuts down the length of the tree and peel the bark off in long strips.

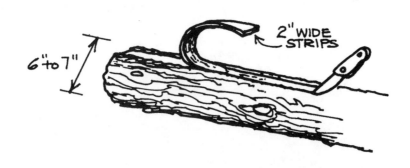

This treehouse has three levels:

1. The ground level platform has two sections - one made from 2x12 lumber and the other made from 3" diameter poles.

2. The second level is accessible by a ladder and has a thatched roof.

3. The third level (the "Crows Nest") which has room for only one brave tree climber.

PLAN

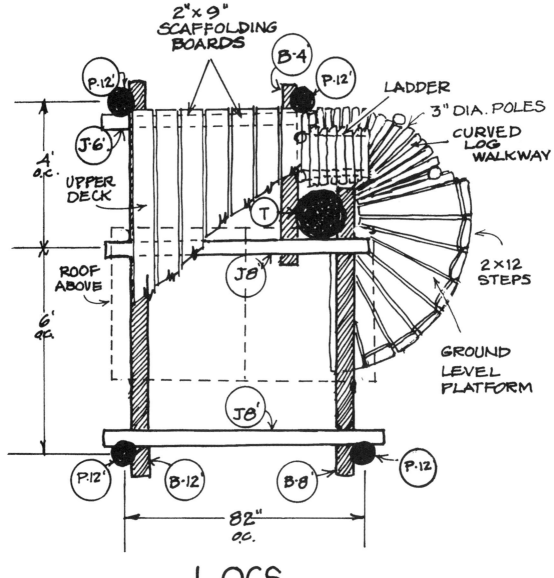

o.c. = on center

LOGS

T = TREE
P = POSTS 6" TO 7" BUTT END, 12' LONG
B = BEAM LOGS 6" DIAMETER
J = JOISTS - 3" x 5" MINI TIES

41

Once you have selected a strong, healthy tree in which to build your treehouse, dig four holes, 30" deep, as shown on the plan. These will hold your four main support poles. Place the poles in the holes and begin backfilling with dirt, making sure to check that the posts are plumb (vertical). Use a 2x4 to compact the soil as you backfill and top it off with a concrete collar. Use one 80 lb. bag of *Sacrete* for each hole and mix it with just enough water to make a stiff consistancy.

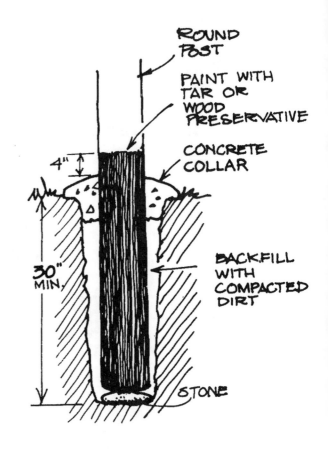

ROUND POST

PAINT WITH TAR OR WOOD PRESERVATIVE

CONCRETE COLLAR

4"

BACKFILL WITH COMPACTED DIRT

30" MIN.

STONE

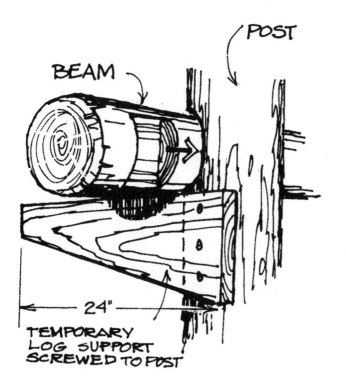

BEAM

POST

24"

TEMPORARY LOG SUPPORT SCREWED TO POST

Attach the three horizontal support beams marked "B" on the plan (and shown shaded), to the posts, six feet above the ground (assuming the ground is level). To do this, it will be necessary to make flat notches on both the post and the beam. Since it will require a lot of cutting and fitting, screw a temporary beam support to the post, as shown here.

Making Log Joints

Making a good connection where two logs meet is crucial in log construction. Never omit this step because unless the logs are notched to fit together, they will roll around and make the treehouse wobbly.

Properly executed, the two logs should "bite" each other like two jaws and almost hold together without screws or rope.

Use the same type of joint on the ladder and on the railings.

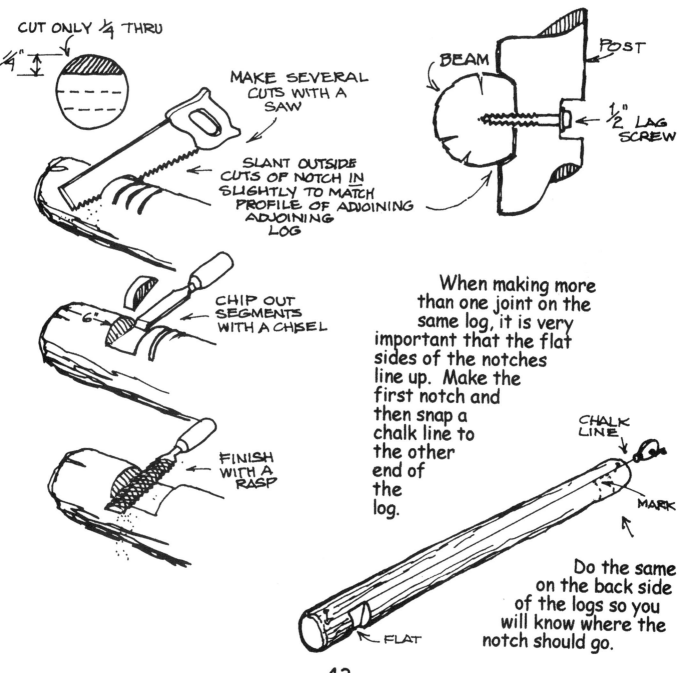

CUT ONLY ¼ THRU

¼"

MAKE SEVERAL CUTS WITH A SAW

SLANT OUTSIDE CUTS OF NOTCH IN SLIGHTLY TO MATCH PROFILE OF ADJOINING ADJOINING LOG

BEAM

POST

½" LAG SCREW

CHIP OUT SEGMENTS WITH A CHISEL

6"

FINISH WITH A RASP

When making more than one joint on the same log, it is very important that the flat sides of the notches line up. Make the first notch and then snap a chalk line to the other end of the log.

CHALK LINE

MARK

Do the same on the back side of the logs so you will know where the notch should go.

FLAT

43

Hammer the logs together so they fit tightly. To hold them together while you drill the holes, tie them with rope.

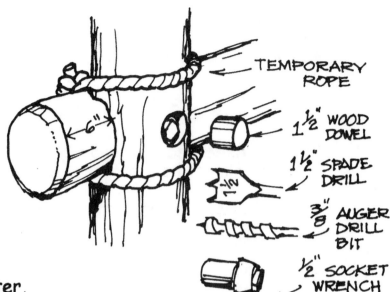

TEMPORARY ROPE

1 1/2" WOOD DOWEL

1 1/2" SPADE DRILL

3/8" AUGER DRILL BIT

1/2" SOCKET WRENCH

Drill a 1 1/2" diameter hole, 1 3/4" deep. Drill a second hole, 3/8" diameter, as a pilot hole for the lag screw. Use a hammer and a socket wrench to screw a 1/2" diameter lag screw into both logs. The length of the lag screws depends on the thickness of the logs. The lag screws should penetrate at least 2" into the second log.

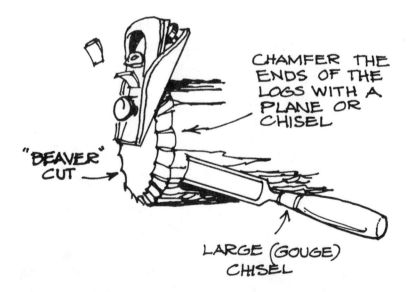

CHAMFER THE ENDS OF THE LOGS WITH A PLANE OR CHISEL

"BEAVER" CUT

LARGE (GOUGE) CHISEL

For an interesting look, round off (chamfer) the ends of the logs, using either a plane or a scoop type chisel called a "gouge". When done right, it should look like a beaver chewed the end of the log.

FRAME

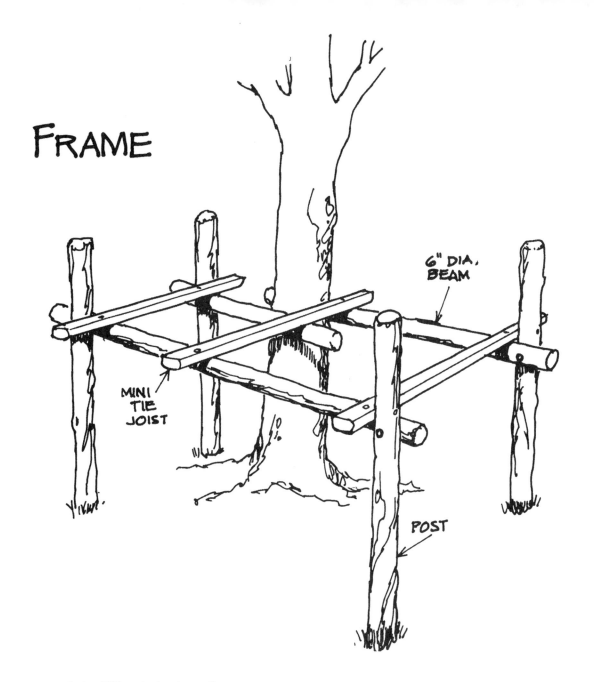

6" DIA. BEAM

MINI TIE JOIST

POST

Use 3 'x 5" mini-ties for
the joists that support
the floor boards, because mini-
ties have two flat sides. Make sure
that they are level before you screw them down to
the beam logs. Mini-ties are pressure-treated and can be bought
at building supply centers or nurseries.

For the floor boards, we recommend 2"x9"x13' long
scaffolding staging planks. They will easily span six feet
without support from underneath. If you want to use standard
2x6 decking instead, increase the amount of mini-tie joists
to one every two feet.

The Ground Level Platform

The first section requires eight pieces of 2x12 lumber, each 4' long, cut diagonally from a 16' board.

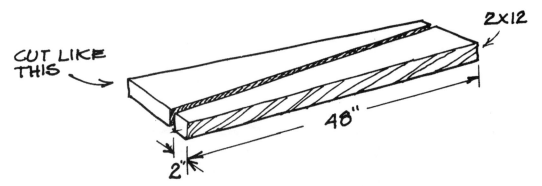

CUT LIKE THIS →

2x12

48"

2"

Assemble the pieces in a semi-circle, allowing a 1" space between each piece.

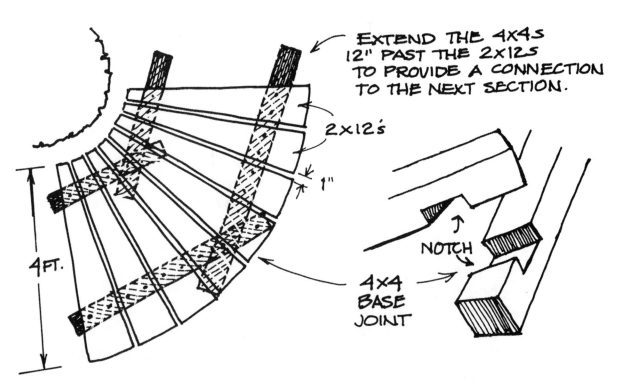

EXTEND THE 4x4s 12" PAST THE 2x12s TO PROVIDE A CONNECTION TO THE NEXT SECTION.

2x12's

1"

4 FT.

4x4 BASE JOINT

NOTCH

To support the platform pieces, cut 4x4 pressure treated beams to serve as a base. Notch them where they intersect and screw the 2x12 pieces to the 4x4s.

The next level is similar to the first level only it uses 3"
diameter cedar poles instead of 2x12 lumber. Cedar poles are
sold at most nursery supply centers. You will need approximately
16 pieces, 3 ft. long. Taper them so they lie close together in a
semi-circle. The poles are screwed sideways to each other and
then screwed to 4x4s underneath.

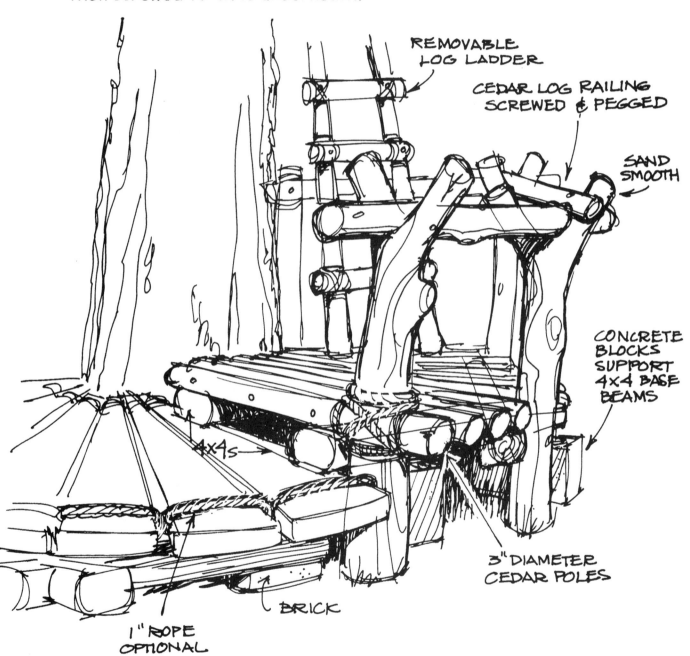

REMOVABLE
LOG LADDER

CEDAR LOG RAILING
SCREWED & PEGGED

SAND
SMOOTH

CONCRETE
BLOCKS
SUPPORT
4X4 BASE
BEAMS

3" DIAMETER
CEDAR POLES

4X4s

BRICK

1" ROPE
OPTIONAL

LASHINGS

Although the rope on this treehouse is for decorative purposes only, it gives the appearance of a treehouse made under survival conditions.

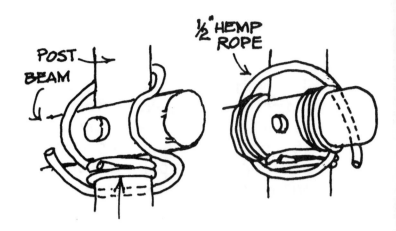

POST
BEAM
½" HEMP ROPE

1. Tie a clove hitch under the beam.

2. Make four turns up in front of the beam, over and behind the post, then down in front of the beam, and around in back of the post.

3. Tighten the lashing by making several turns around the intersection of the two poles and finish with a final clove hitch at the top.

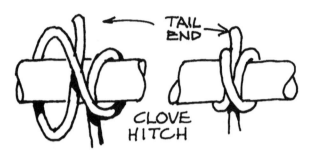

TAIL END

CLOVE HITCH

YOU CAN TELL IF YOU TIED IT CORRECTLY IF YOU SEE THE TAIL END OF THE ROPE STICKING OUT BETWEEN THE TWO TURNS.

CROWS NEST

Use a half barrel sold at most nurseries. Sand the inside, using a 3" electric sander, and apply several coats of poly.

Drill several holes in the bottom to drain any rain water and drill two or three holes at the top to tie ropes to. This will be helpful when you hoist it up into the tree. Use rope to tie the crow's nest to the tree and attach support brackets, for additional support.

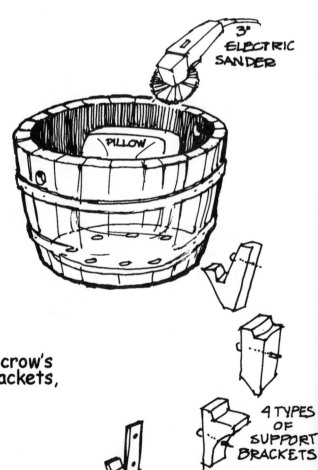

3" ELECTRIC SANDER

PILLOW

4 TYPES OF SUPPORT BRACKETS

ROOF
Bamboo
&
Thatch

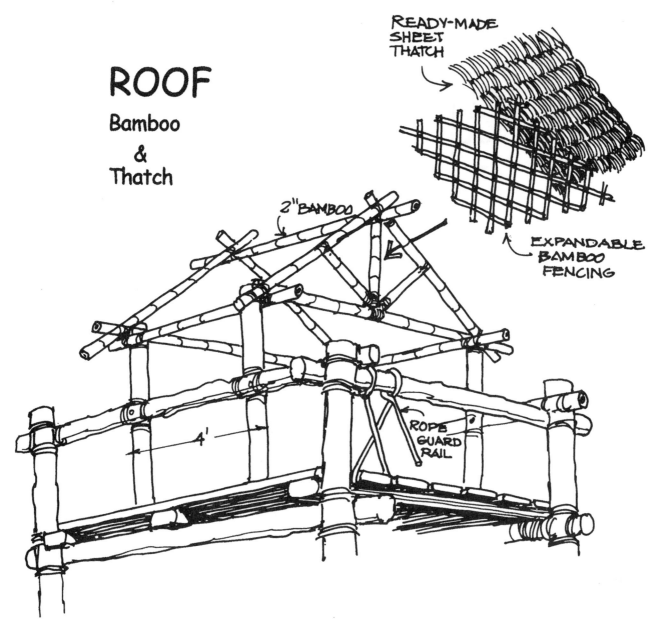

READY-MADE SHEET THATCH

2" BAMBOO

EXPANDABLE BAMBOO FENCING

ROPE GUARD RAIL

4'

Make the railing out of 3" diameter cedar poles (also bought at a nursery). Make the rope guard rail out of 3/4" hemp rope, as shown above.

Build a bamboo frame, using 2" bamboo, held together with screws and special bamboo (black) string.

Cover the roof with expandable bamboo fencing and ready-made thatch sheets, found at most nursery centers or by calling (800) 229 2263. Use plastic-coated wire to attach the fencing material and the thatching to the bamboo frame.

Huts and Forts

FORT APACHE

LOOK-OUT TOWER

This twenty-one foot tall tower is perfect for a look-out on top of a hill to spy on the approaching enemy. In 1776, George Washington had one built in Summit, New Jersey (my hometown) to observe any British troops that might be marching from New York. In case they were spotted, a rider would be dispatched immediately to Washington's headquarters in Morristown, N.J. to alert the troops.

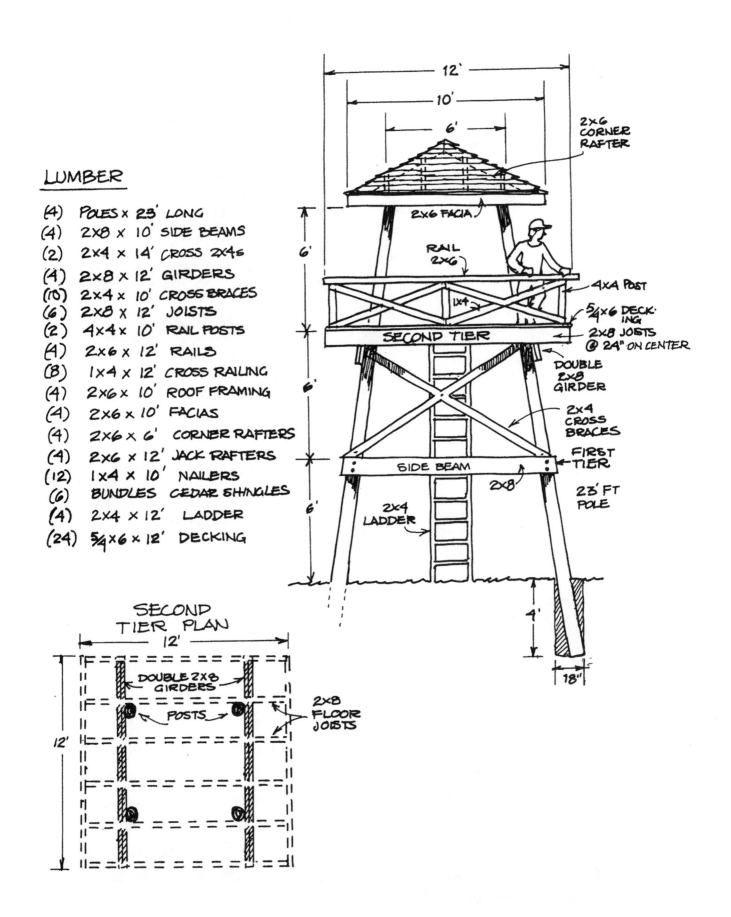

LUMBER

- (4) POLES x 23' LONG
- (4) 2x8 x 10' SIDE BEAMS
- (2) 2x4 x 14' CROSS 2x4s
- (4) 2x8 x 12' GIRDERS
- (10) 2x4 x 10' CROSS BRACES
- (6) 2x8 x 12' JOISTS
- (2) 4x4 x 10' RAIL POSTS
- (4) 2x6 x 12' RAILS
- (8) 1x4 x 12' CROSS RAILING
- (4) 2x6 x 10' ROOF FRAMING
- (4) 2x6 x 10' FACIAS
- (4) 2x6 x 6' CORNER RAFTERS
- (4) 2x6 x 12' JACK RAFTERS
- (12) 1x4 x 10' NAILERS
- (6) BUNDLES CEDAR SHINGLES
- (4) 2x4 x 12' LADDER
- (24) 5/4 x 6 x 12' DECKING

12'
10'
6'

2x6 CORNER RAFTER

2x6 FACIA

RAIL 2x6

1x4

SECOND TIER

4x4 POST

5/4 x 6 DECKING

2x8 JOISTS @ 24" ON CENTER

DOUBLE 2x8 GIRDER

2x4 CROSS BRACES

FIRST TIER

23' FT POLE

SIDE BEAM

2x8

2x4 LADDER

6'
6'
6'

4'

18"

SECOND TIER PLAN

12'

12'

DOUBLE 2x8 GIRDERS

POSTS

2x8 FLOOR JOISTS

To make this tower, you will need four sturdy poles, measuring 10" at the bottom, tapering to 6" at the top. Depending on where you live, you might be able to find them in the woods or you might be able to get used telephone poles from your local telephone company.

If you are cutting down live trees, make sure to get permission first. The best trees to use are pine trees, because they grow straight and are easy to peel in the spring. The butt ends should be soaked in wood preservative and painted with asphalt roofing cement (tar) before inserting them in the ground.

IF THE POLES ARE FRESH CUT, THEY WILL BE HEAVY AND WILL REQUIRE THREE OR FOUR STRONG PEOPLE TO CARRY THEM.

2X4s

NOTCH TO
FIT BIKES

If strong volunteers are not available, you might try to carry the logs by tying three 2x4s across two bicycles and lashing the the log between two bikes. Notice that the bikes are pulled backwards.

Dig four holes for the poles 11' 6" apart and 48" deep. Use a post hole digger or a shovel and make the holes 18" in diameter.

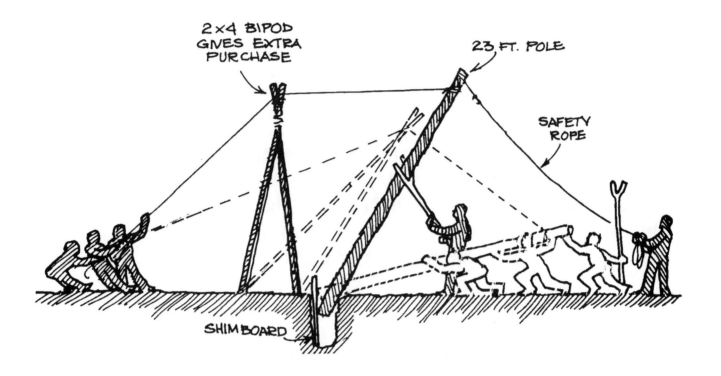

To make it easier to raise the poles, rig up a bipod (as shown in the above sketch) made from two, 16' long, pieces of 2x4. Have two teams of kids - one to start pushing up the log and the other to pull it up the final distance. You should also have two assistants with 12' long forked poles to support the larger pole as it goes up. (Perhaps these should be two adults.) Work together as a team with only one person giving orders. (Perhaps you!)

This can be a lot of fun if you make it into a pole raising party with refreshments at the end.

NOTE:
Once the poles are in their holes, do not fill the holes with dirt until you have completed the next two steps. Temporarily brace the poles with 2x4s, to hold them in place.

Step 1

Lean the poles in towards the center. Measure up about 6 ft. and mark. This will be where your first side beams will go. Screw four 2x8s, 10' long, to the logs so they meet at the outside corners. Use 1/2" x 5" lag screws to attach them. Make sure the beams are level.

TIP : Put only one lag screw in the end of each side beam, Wait until the whole structure is level, plumb and square, and then put in the second lag screw.

Measure the diagonal distances between two opposites sets of poles, The measurements should be the same. If they are not, put some rope around the poles and pull them one way or another until the diagonals measure the same. Then nail two 2x4s across the poles to hold them in place.

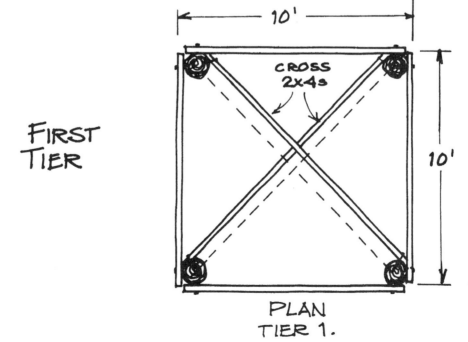

FIRST
TIER

CROSS
2x4s

10'

10'

PLAN
TIER 1.

Step 2

The second tier is slightly different because it supports the floor of the tower. As before, measure up another 6' on the poles and mark. Nail two 2x8 beams together on two sides. Allow the beams to extend 24" on each end. Use the side beams below to stand on or use a 10' long ladder.

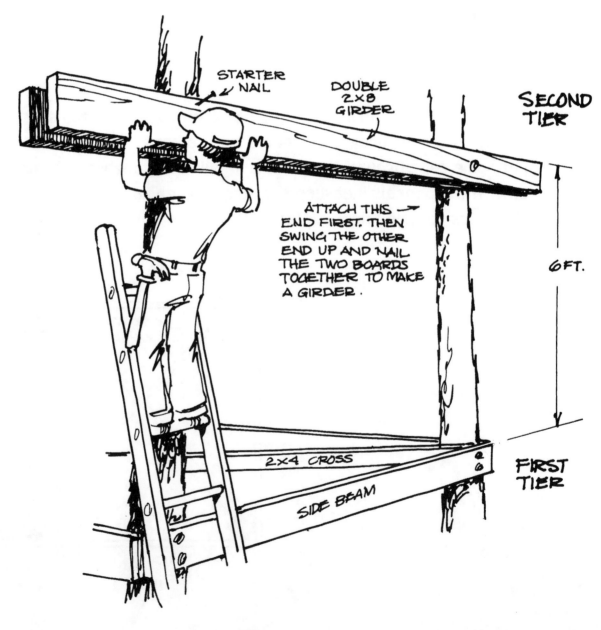

STARTER NAIL

DOUBLE 2X8 GIRDER

SECOND TIER

ATTACH THIS END FIRST. THEN SWING THE OTHER END UP AND NAIL THE TWO BOARDS TOGETHER TO MAKE A GIRDER.

6 FT.

2X4 CROSS

SIDE BEAM

FIRST TIER

Step 3

Once the second tier girders are fastened in place, nail 2x4 cross braces diagonally between poles, as in step 1.

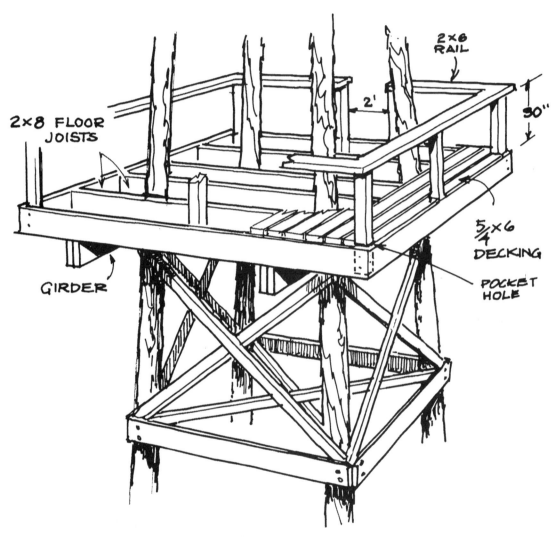

Nail 2x8 floor joists over girders, 24" on center.
Nail 5/4 x 6 deck boards over the joists.

Cut 3 1/2" x 3 1/2" pocket holes through the decking at each corner, to fit the 4x4 railing posts, and screw them in place. Use 2x6s for the top rail, allowing a 2' wide opening on one side, for access.

Step 4 - Roof

Build the roof 6 ft. above
the second tier by attaching
four pieces of 2x6 x10 ft.
to the tops of the posts.
To install them at the
same level, you will have
to cut notches out of each
piece where they intersect.

Next, cut four, 6 ft. long, facia
boards and nail them to the
ends of the roof framing beams.
Cut four, 6 ft. long, ridge boards
to go from the top of the roof to the
corners.

Once the roof is completely framed,
nail the 1x4 nailers (spaced sheathing)
on at 5 1/2" on center. Nail 18" cedar
shingles to the nailers. For a truly
professional job, cut and weave a top
row of shingles over the four ridges.

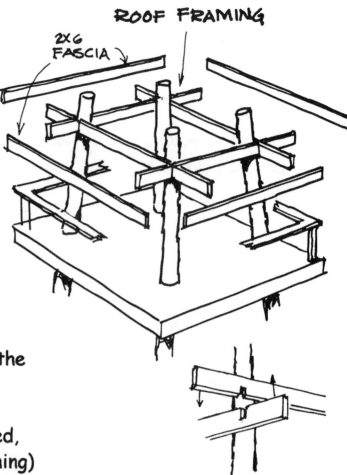

ROOF FRAMING

2X6 FASCIA

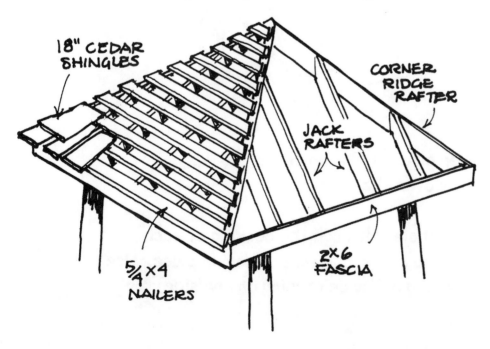

18" CEDAR SHINGLES

CORNER RIDGE RAFTER

JACK RAFTERS

5/4 X4 NAILERS

2X6 FASCIA

JUNK HUT

The saying, "One man's trash is another man's treasure", is especially true for some residents of large cities who have built livable dwellings ("*Casitas*") out of salvaged materials found in abandoned lots. You can build a junk hut too, but you might choose a place to build your hut that is hidden from your neighbors. You don't need a lot of money to build this hut, but you do need ingenuity and resourcefulness. Even junk can be beautiful if it is assembled in a creative way.

Look for building sites where contractors may be throwing away leftover lumber. (Ask before you take.) Visit your lumber yard and ask if they have free scraps they want to get rid of. Most of them do. Ask your neighbors if they have any old boards that they don't want. Don't be timid about asking - you are actually doing a good thing by recycling lumber.

Try and find as many 2x4s as you can for the frame. If the pieces are not long enough, nail several short pieces together to make a longer piece.

Use boards or plywood to cover the roof.

The secret to framing is to plan all your joints in advance. You might even make a small model out of ice cream sticks.

BUILD THE FRONT FRAMES ON THE GROUND. PROP THEM UP AND ADD THE 2X4 RAFTERS TO HOLD THE TWO FRAMES IN PLACE.

(YOU WILL NEED HELP TO DO THIS.)

FRONT FRAME

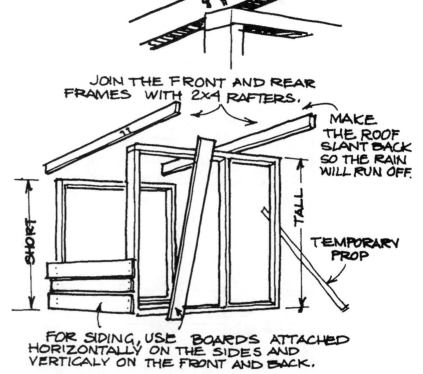

TOENAIL

JOIN THE FRONT AND REAR FRAMES WITH 2X4 RAFTERS.

MAKE THE ROOF SLANT BACK SO THE RAIN WILL RUN OFF.

SHORT

TALL

TEMPORARY PROP

FOR SIDING, USE BOARDS ATTACHED HORIZONTALLY ON THE SIDES AND VERTICALLY ON THE FRONT AND BACK.

Use 2x4s to
frame window
and door openings.

2x4s

Roof

Add more 2x4s to the
roof, if necessary, and
cover with scrap
plywood or boards.

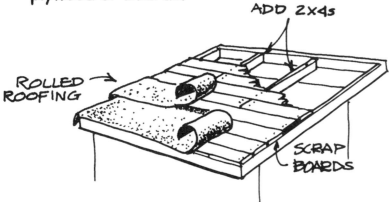

ADD 2x4s

ROLLED →
ROOFING

SCRAP
BOARDS

Cover the boards
with tar paper or
rolled roofing.

Check your local dump to see
if there are any old windows
or doors that have been thrown out.
Carry them home on a wagon.

Mountain Stream Hut

...is a rest stop for hikers and backpackers. It is a place to stop and enjoy the beauty of the wilderness and to fill one's canteen with cool water. Most of the materials can be found in the nearby woods, however, the shakes and nailer boards will probably have to be purchased and carried to the site. With enough help from friends, this hut could be built in a few weekends.

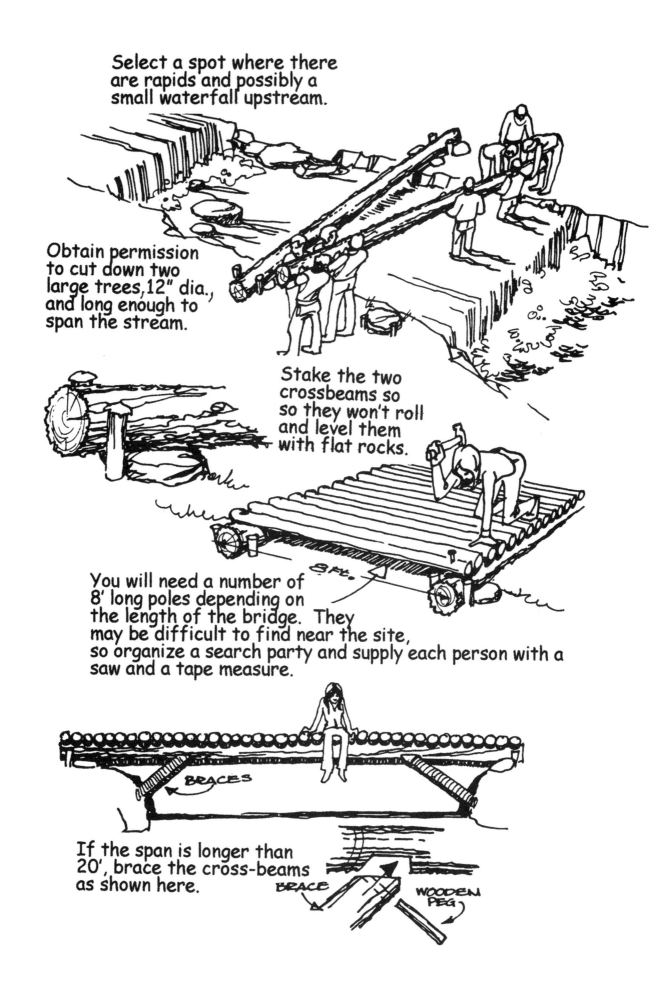

Select a spot where there are rapids and possibly a small waterfall upstream.

Obtain permission to cut down two large trees, 12" dia., and long enough to span the stream.

Stake the two crossbeams so so they won't roll and level them with flat rocks.

You will need a number of 8' long poles depending on the length of the bridge. They may be difficult to find near the site, so organize a search party and supply each person with a saw and a tape measure.

BRACES

If the span is longer than 20', brace the cross-beams as shown here.

BRACE

WOODEN PEG

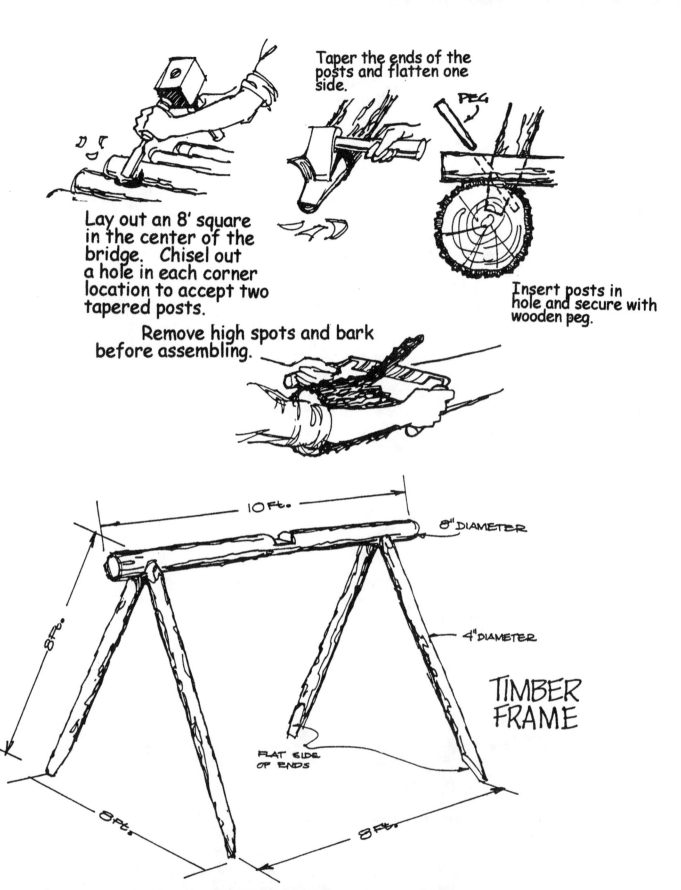

Taper the ends of the posts and flatten one side.

PEG

Lay out an 8' square in the center of the bridge. Chisel out a hole in each corner location to accept two tapered posts.

Insert posts in hole and secure with wooden peg.

Remove high spots and bark before assembling.

10 Ft.

8" DIAMETER

8 Ft.

4" DIAMETER

TIMBER FRAME

FLAT SIDE OF ENDS

8 Ft.

8 Ft.

First stage of the frame should look like this. Make sure the flattened sides of the posts face in so they will interface with the ends of the posts in the second stage.

Construct the next two gables as shown below. Note that all the poles are the same length (8 ft.) with the exception of the two ridge poles which extend 1 ft. on each end.

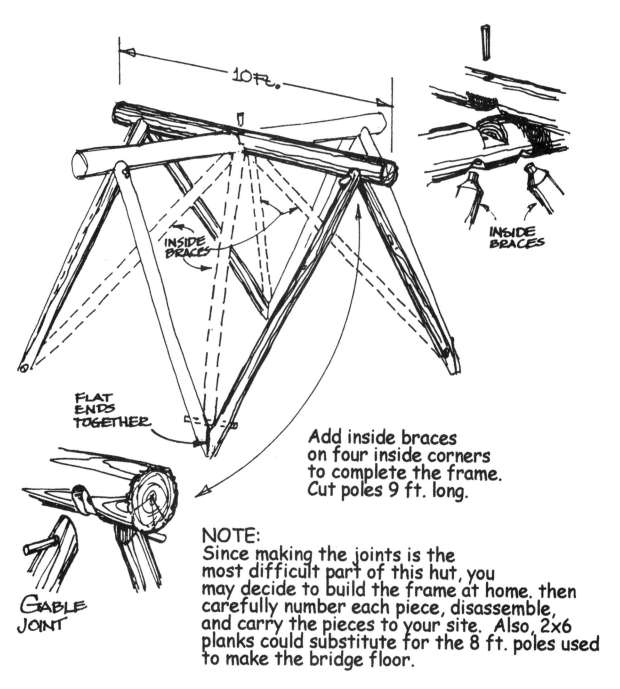

10 ft.

INSIDE BRACES

INSIDE BRACES

FLAT ENDS TOGETHER

GABLE JOINT

Add inside braces on four inside corners to complete the frame. Cut poles 9 ft. long.

NOTE:
Since making the joints is the most difficult part of this hut, you may decide to build the frame at home. then carefully number each piece, disassemble, and carry the pieces to your site. Also, 2x6 planks could substitute for the 8 ft. poles used to make the bridge floor.

Use cedar for the posts since it is light and easier to carry.

65

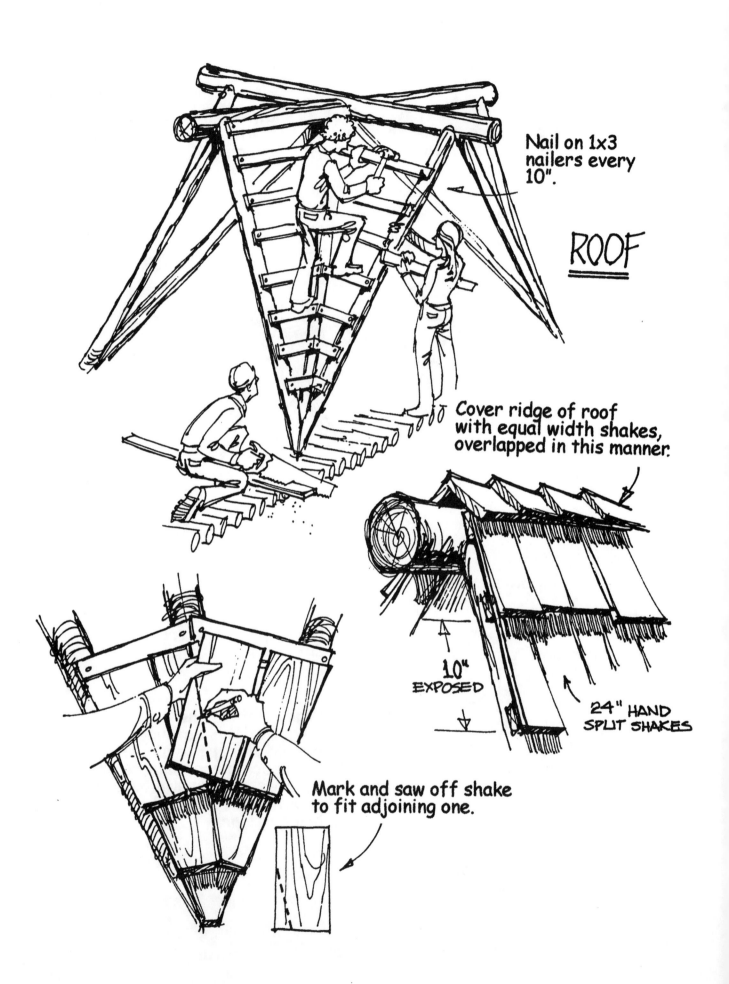

Nail on 1x3 nailers every 10".

ROOF

Cover ridge of roof with equal width shakes, overlapped in this manner.

10" EXPOSED

24" HAND SPLIT SHAKES

Mark and saw off shake to fit adjoining one.

LEAN-TO

To build this lean-to you will need lots of trees, time, and friends. The wall logs are placed vertically, rather than horizontally as in the traditional Adirondack style, to allow the rain to run down instead of around the logs, which can trap the water between them.

This lean-to is not intended to keep you warm. In fact, space is left between the wall logs to allow for air infiltration. Its purpose is to provide overhead protection from the rain. Face the open end of the lean-to south to allow sunlight inside.

* For plans on how to build a traditional Adirondack lean-to, read our book, *Rustic Retreats,* and see www.stilesdesigns.com.

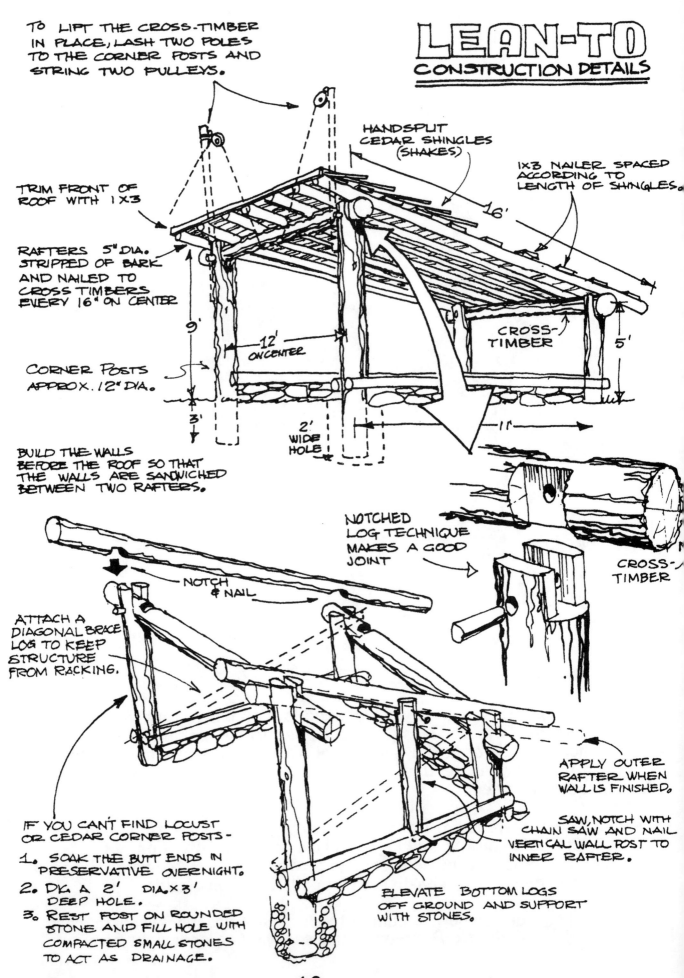

TO LIFT THE CROSS-TIMBER IN PLACE, LASH TWO POLES TO THE CORNER POSTS AND STRING TWO PULLEYS.

LEAN-TO
CONSTRUCTION DETAILS

HANDSPLIT CEDAR SHINGLES (SHAKES)

1X3 NAILER SPACED ACCORDING TO LENGTH OF SHINGLES.

TRIM FRONT OF ROOF WITH 1X3

16'

RAFTERS 5" DIA. STRIPPED OF BARK AND NAILED TO CROSS TIMBERS EVERY 16" ON CENTER

CROSS-TIMBER

9'

5'

CORNER POSTS APPROX. 12" DIA.

12' ON CENTER

3'

2' WIDE HOLE

11'

BUILD THE WALLS BEFORE THE ROOF SO THAT THE WALLS ARE SANDWICHED BETWEEN TWO RAFTERS.

NOTCHED LOG TECHNIQUE MAKES A GOOD JOINT

CROSS-TIMBER

NOTCH & NAIL

ATTACH A DIAGONAL BRACE LOG TO KEEP STRUCTURE FROM RACKING.

APPLY OUTER RAFTER WHEN WALL IS FINISHED.

SAW, NOTCH WITH CHAIN SAW AND NAIL VERTICAL WALL POST TO INNER RAFTER.

IF YOU CAN'T FIND LOCUST OR CEDAR CORNER POSTS -

1. SOAK THE BUTT ENDS IN PRESERVATIVE OVERNIGHT.
2. DIG A 2' DIA. X 3' DEEP HOLE.
3. REST POST ON ROUNDED STONE AND FILL HOLE WITH COMPACTED SMALL STONES TO ACT AS DRAINAGE.

ELEVATE BOTTOM LOGS OFF GROUND AND SUPPORT WITH STONES.

FoRT BrAvo

This fort looks best if it is made out of cedar posts and poles. You can find cedar posts at fence suppliers and cedar poles at landscape supply yards. You will need:

- (4) cedar posts, 6"-8" diameter, 14' long (corner posts)
- (2) cedar posts, 5" diameter, 8' long (side support beams)
- (4) mini 3"x5" landscape ties, 8' long (floor joists)
- (9) 2x8 Douglas fir boards, 7' long (floor boards)
- (8) cedar poles, 4" diameter, 8' long (rails)
- (38) cedar poles, 3" diameter, 33" long (vertical railing posts)
- (4) cedar posts, 4" diameter, 7' long (roof support beams)
- (8) cedar poles, 3" diameter, 2' long (roof braces)
- (8) cedar poles, 3"-4" diameter, 5' long (roof rafters)

The roof materials depend on whether you want to use cedar shakes or asphalt shingles (see pages 58 and 37 for details). The shutters are optional.

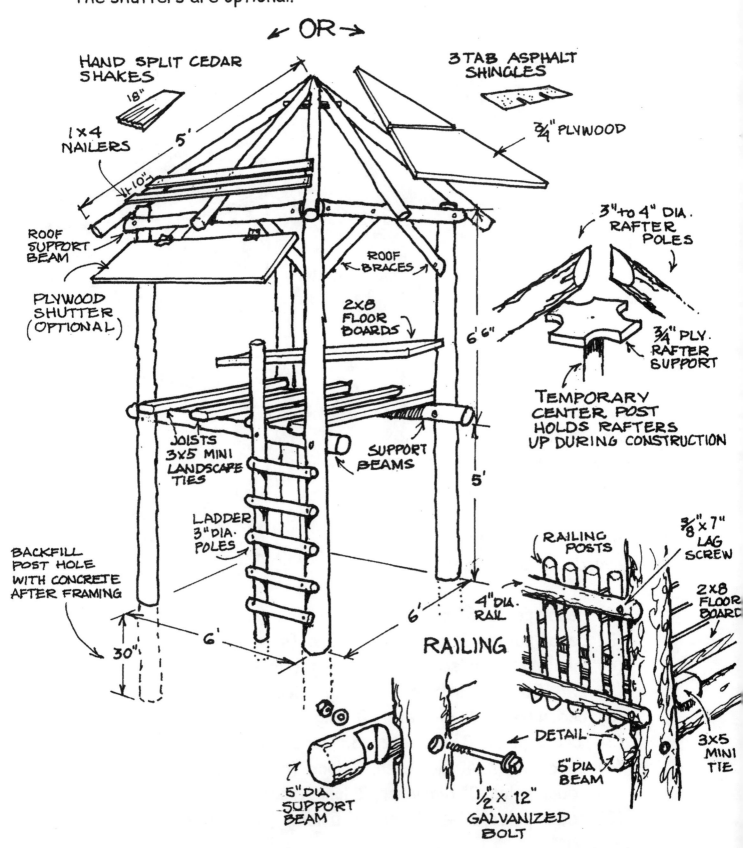

OR

HAND SPLIT CEDAR SHAKES

18"

1×4 NAILERS

5'

4"-10"

ROOF SUPPORT BEAM

PLYWOOD SHUTTER (OPTIONAL)

BACKFILL POST HOLE WITH CONCRETE AFTER FRAMING

30"

6'

JOISTS 3×5 MINI LANDSCAPE TIES

LADDER 3" DIA. POLES

ROOF BRACES

2×8 FLOOR BOARDS

SUPPORT BEAMS

3 TAB ASPHALT SHINGLES

3/4" PLYWOOD

6' 6"

6'

5'

3" TO 4" DIA. RAFTER POLES

3/4" PLY. RAFTER SUPPORT

TEMPORARY CENTER POST HOLDS RAFTERS UP DURING CONSTRUCTION

RAILING POSTS

3/8" × 7" LAG SCREW

2×8 FLOOR BOARD

4" DIA. RAIL

RAILING

DETAIL

5" DIA. SUPPORT BEAM

1/2" × 12" GALVANIZED BOLT

5" DIA BEAM

3×5 MINI TIE

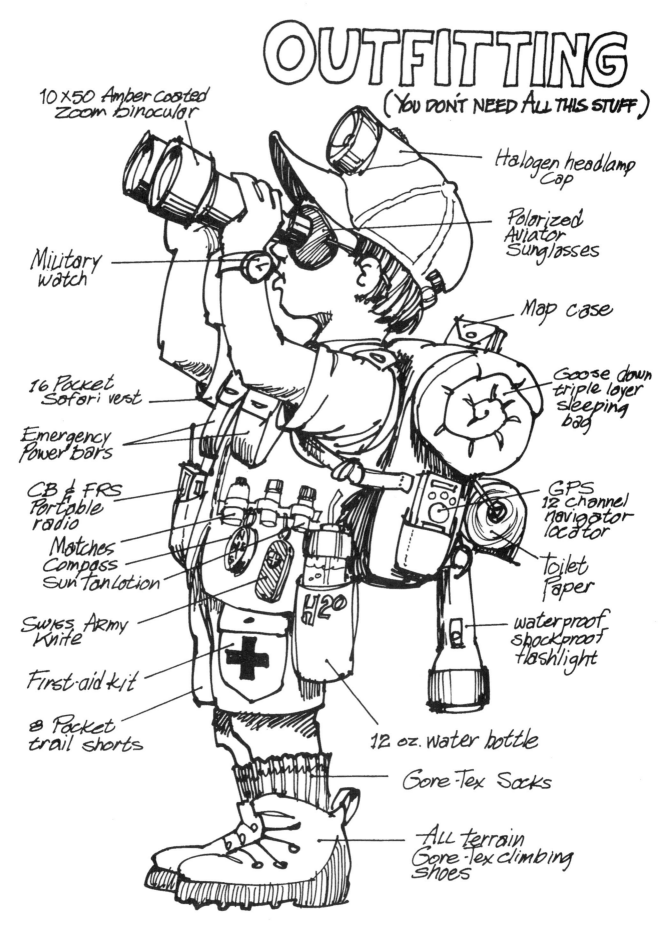

Camping out Overnight

Planning on camping out overnight in your hut? Here is a list of things you might bring along:

1.   **Flashlight or Lantern**

Check to make sure that your batteries are fresh.
Don't bring candles or kerosene lanterns as they could start a fire.

2.   **Cell Phone or Walkie Talkie**

Now and then you might want to check on your parents to see if they are all right.

3.   **Food and Drinks**

Here is a chance to pig out on all your favorite food, but you might want to surprise Mom by including some healthy snacks as well, like power bars and fruit. Pack all your food in an easy-to-carry cooler and don't forget things like knives, forks spoons and even napkins. Bring along a thermos with ice for your cold drinks.

4. Garbage

Bring along a small plastic garbage bag for leftover food and candy wrappers. Make sure when you leave your hut the next day there is nothing left that squirrels or mice could eat; otherwise you might have some unexpected visitors while you are away.

5. Bedding

Of course, you will take along a sleeping bag or blankets and maybe even a pillow, but what about a mattress? If you are sleeping on a hard floor, you will need something under you, like an inflatable mattress or maybe a cushion from a chaise lounge. Or try hanging a hammock from two hooks on the wall.

6. Clock

Although the birds will probably wake you up in the morning, you might want a clock so you can give yourself time to get to school. Also, it's good to know what time you went to sleep.

7. Insect Spray

Depending on where you live, bugs may, or may not, be a problem. Remember, bugs will be attracted to your flashlight at night, so it might be a good idea to buy some mosquito netting to cover up any openings to the outdoors. While you are at it, the day before you camp out, check for ants and spiders, spray with insecticide, and sweep out the hut to make it ready for your sleep-over.

8. Books and Magazines

In case you can't sleep right away, bring something to read, or better yet, bring a pad and paper and write about how you feel camping out alone. The first time you try camping, you might find it a little scary the moment you turn out the light, but be brave. Think about how tough you are and remember, it's really not that much different from sleeping in your own home - just different surroundings. You will wake up the next morning proud of yourself and ready to tell your friends about your experience.

CATAPULT

This adaptation of the ancient catapult uses only harmless snowballs in the winter and soft styrofoam balls in the summer for ammunition. It can be made in an hour, using materials found around the house.

Materials:

- (1) 3/4" thick plywood, 12" x 12"
- (1) 1/2" x 2" board, 24" long
- (1) 2x8 board, 16" long
- (1) 3/4" dowel, 10" long
- (3) 3/4" dowels, 2" long
- (1) piece heavy string, 36" long
- (1) 1" wide rubber band, 8" long
     (cut from a car tire inner tube)
- (1) empty tuna fish can
- (3) #6, 3/8" long screws

In case of a snowball attack, one must always be prepared, and this snowball launcher is just what is needed to protect a snow fort.

Step 1
Cut a piece of 3/4"
plywood in half,
across the diagonal,
to form two triangles.
Round off the corners.

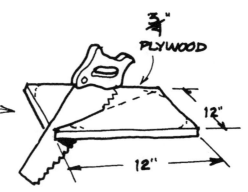

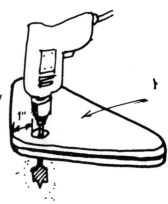

Step 2
Drill a 3/4" diameter
hole through both pieces,
1" from the top.

Step 3
File and sand the
dowel so that it turns
easily in the holes.

3/4" x 9 1/4" DOWEL

Step 4
Nail the plywood sides to
the 2x8, 16" long base.
Make a 2" long flat surface
on the dowel for the "arm".

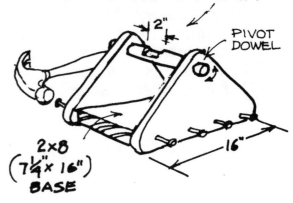

PIVOT DOWEL

2x8
(7 1/4" x 16")
BASE

Step 5
Cut a 1 1/2" wide section
from an old inner tube.

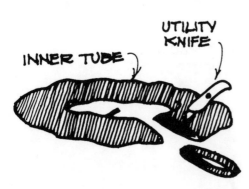

INNER TUBE

UTILITY KNIFE

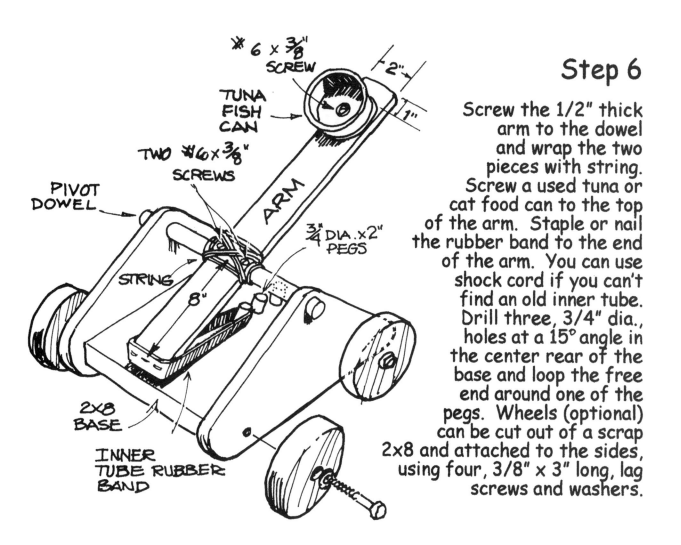

#6 X 3/8" SCREW

TUNA FISH CAN

TWO #6 X 3/8" SCREWS

PIVOT DOWEL

ARM

2"

1"

3/4" DIA. X 2" PEGS

STRING

8"

2X8 BASE

INNER TUBE RUBBER BAND

Step 6

Screw the 1/2" thick arm to the dowel and wrap the two pieces with string. Screw a used tuna or cat food can to the top of the arm. Staple or nail the rubber band to the end of the arm. You can use shock cord if you can't find an old inner tube. Drill three, 3/4" dia., holes at a 15° angle in the center rear of the base and loop the free end around one of the pegs. Wheels (optional) can be cut out of a scrap 2x8 and attached to the sides, using four, 3/8" x 3" long, lag screws and washers.

Step 7

To operate the catapult, place a ball in the can, pull back the arm with your other hand and let go, allowing the arm to snap forward, projecting the ball into the air.

WARNING: Do not use baseballs or anything hard that could hurt someone. To increase distance, move the rubber band back to the next peg.

SECTION

Treasure Chest

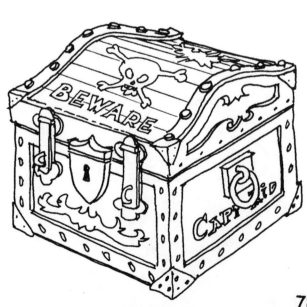

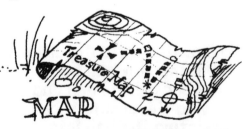

MAP

Draw the map with brown ink on tan grocery bag paper. Carefully tear the edges to make it look worn. Seal the map with red candle wax and hide it in a secret place.

What to put in a treasure chest

If you are using the treasure chest for a treasure hunt, you can load it up with chocolate coins and cookies; however, if you leave it underground for more than a day, don't stock it with anything perishable. Instead, make fake coins by cutting off disks from a wooden dowel and painting them gold, or fill it with jewelry made out of glass beads and aluminum foil.

Parents - Consider making this the *real thing* by burying rare coins or copper pennies. In the near future, copper pennies may become obsolete and in time increase in value.

Suggestion

Great for Birthday Parties

Make a map for each guest by copying the master map using tan paper in a copy machine. Attach a clue directing each guest to the first secret location, i.e. mail box, trash can, cat bowl, etc. At each location leave a clue to the next location, such as "I look at you each morning while you are brushing your teeth" (bathroom mirror). The last clue on the map should show two coordinates that intersect over the buried treasure.

NOTE: Accurately measure these two distances with a tape measure and record them in a safe place. (Some treasure chests, like the one we made, have been lost forever.)

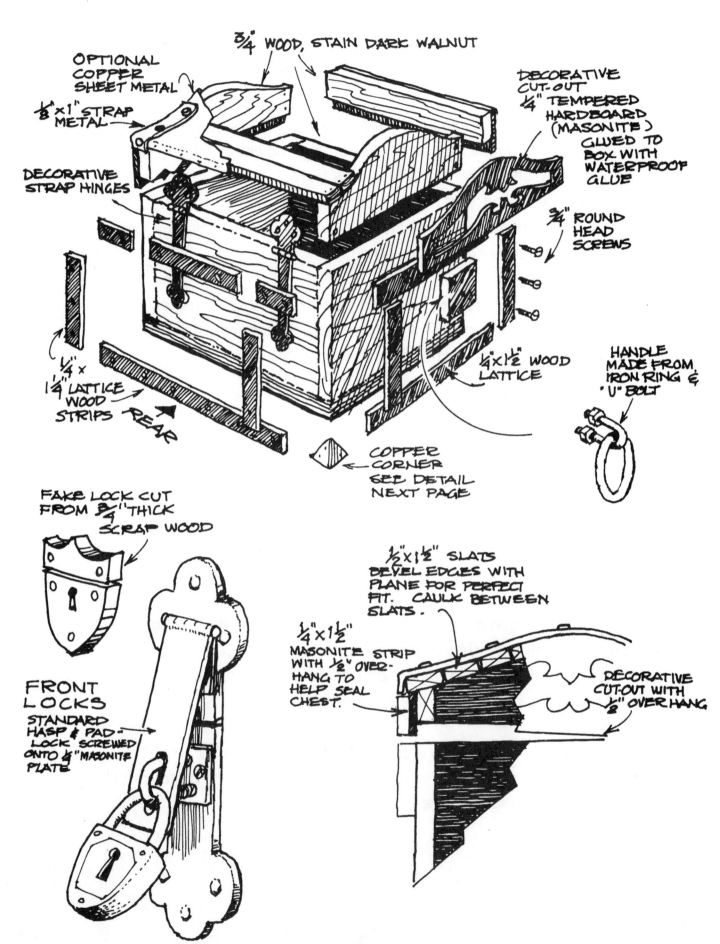

OPTIONAL COPPER SHEET METAL

⅛"x1" STRAP METAL

¾" WOOD, STAIN DARK WALNUT

DECORATIVE STRAP HINGES

DECORATIVE CUT-OUT ¼" TEMPERED HARDBOARD (MASONITE) GLUED TO BOX WITH WATERPROOF GLUE

¾" ROUND HEAD SCREWS

¼" x 1¼" LATTICE WOOD STRIPS REAR

¼" x 1½" WOOD LATTICE

HANDLE MADE FROM IRON RING & "U" BOLT

COPPER CORNER SEE DETAIL NEXT PAGE

FAKE LOCK CUT FROM ¾" THICK SCRAP WOOD

½" x 1½" SLATS BEVEL EDGES WITH PLANE FOR PERFECT FIT. CAULK BETWEEN SLATS.

¼" x 1½" MASONITE STRIP WITH ½" OVER-HANG TO HELP SEAL CHEST.

DECORATIVE CUT-OUT WITH ½" OVERHANG

FRONT LOCKS

STANDARD HASP & PAD-LOCK SCREWED ONTO ⅛" MASONITE PLATE

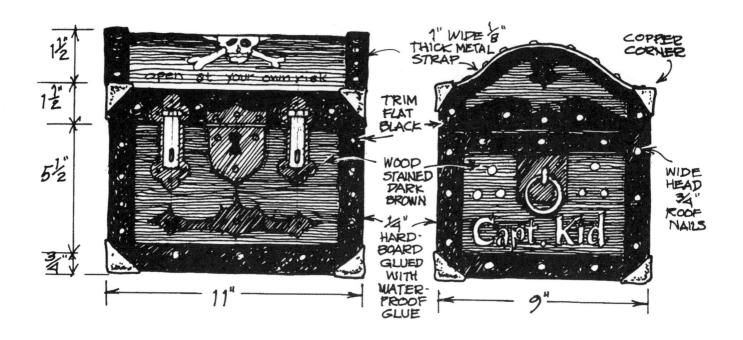

1 1/2"

1 1/2"

5 1/2"

3/4"

11"

9"

open at your own risk

Capt. Kid

1" WIDE 1/8" THICK METAL STRAP

COPPER CORNER

TRIM FLAT BLACK

WOOD STAINED DARK BROWN

1/4" HARD-BOARD GLUED WITH WATER-PROOF GLUE

WIDE HEAD 3/4" ROOF NAILS

COPPER CORNERS

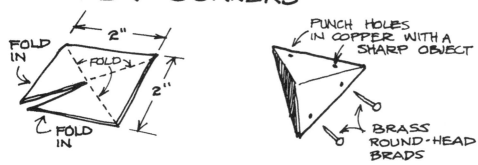

FOLD IN

2"

FOLD

2"

FOLD IN

PUNCH HOLES IN COPPER WITH A SHARP OBJECT

BRASS ROUND-HEAD BRADS

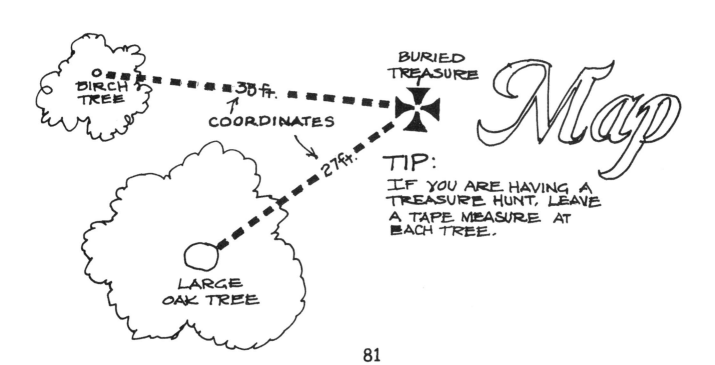

0 BIRCH TREE

30 ft.

COORDINATES

BURIED TREASURE

27 ft.

LARGE OAK TREE

Map

TIP:

IF YOU ARE HAVING A TREASURE HUNT, LEAVE A TAPE MEASURE AT EACH TREE.

Cannon

This authentic looking cannon looks terrifyingly real but actually only shoots a soft "nerf" ball about ten feet. If the firing mechanism seems too involved to make, you can eliminate it and still use the cannon as an historical relic. A cannon like this looks perfect in any kid's fort or treehouse.

Making the barrel of the cannon is very simple. At your plumbing supply store, ask them to cut you two pieces of 4" PVC drain pipe, one 10 1/2" long and the other 12" long. Also buy a 4" i.d. PVC glue cap, two 4" i.d. PVC couplings, and a small can of PVC cement. With a hand saw cut 2 1/2" off one of the couplings to fit on the front of the cannon muzzle. Glue the pieces together, as shown in the illustrations. If you are a perfectionist, bevel all the exposed edges of pipe *before* you glue them together, using a belt sander and coarse sandpaper.

Build the base using 2x3s for the sides and 3/4" plywood for the floor. Cut the wheels and the two barrel support pieces from 2x6 lumber. Cut and screw the 2x3s together and screw them to the double pieces of plywood from underneath. Attach the sides to the support pieces using four, 4"long, 1/4" lag screws. Cut the 1 1/4" diameter poles for the axles, allowing 1 1/2" to extend past the wheels. Allow 1/8" clearance for the wheels to turn without rubbing on the sides. Bore the holes slightly larger than the axle wheels so the wheels can turn freely. Screw the axle poles to the bottom of the plywood base. To strengthen the joints, cut four 12" wood shim strips at 45 degrees and glue them to both sides of the axles. Bore 1/4" holes near the end of the axles and insert the retaining pegs.

To make it look really authentic, screw an old brass door knob onto the end of the barrel.

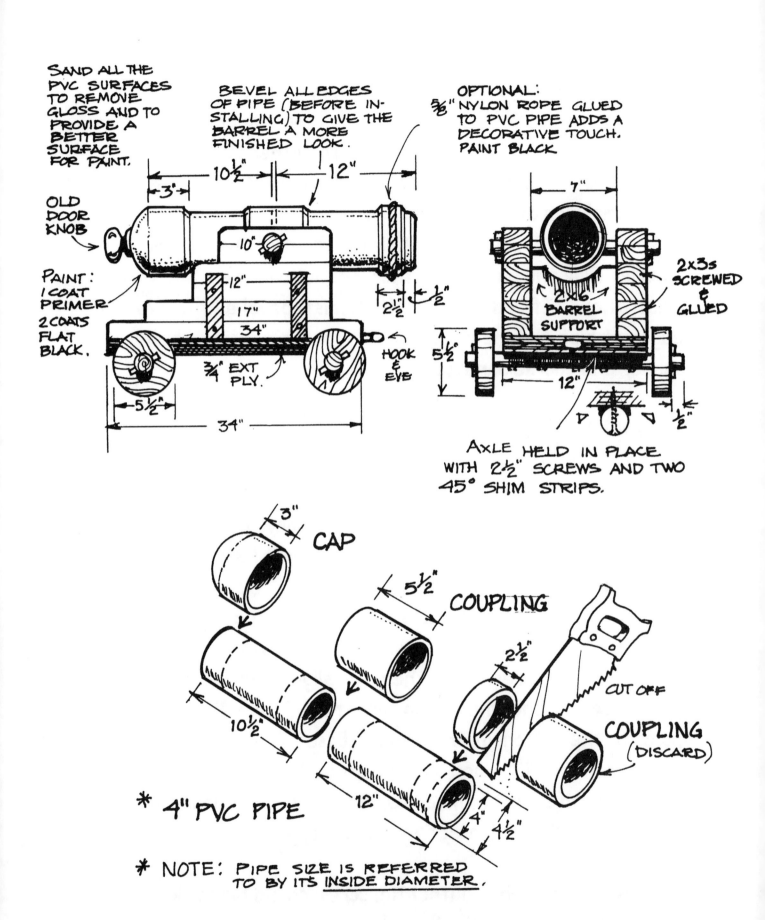

SAND ALL THE PVC SURFACES TO REMOVE GLOSS AND TO PROVIDE A BETTER SURFACE FOR PAINT.

BEVEL ALL EDGES OF PIPE (BEFORE INSTALLING) TO GIVE THE BARREL A MORE FINISHED LOOK.

OPTIONAL: 5/8" NYLON ROPE GLUED TO PVC PIPE ADDS A DECORATIVE TOUCH. PAINT BLACK

OLD DOOR KNOB

PAINT: 1 COAT PRIMER 2 COATS FLAT BLACK.

10 1/2"

3"

12"

10"

12"

17"

34"

2 1/2"

1/2"

3/4" EXT PLY.

HOOK & EYE

5 1/2"

34"

7"

2×6 BARREL SUPPORT

2×3s SCREWED & GLUED

5 1/2"

12"

1/2"

AXLE HELD IN PLACE WITH 2 1/2" SCREWS AND TWO 45° SHIM STRIPS.

3"

CAP

5 1/2"

COUPLING

2 1/2"

CUT OFF

COUPLING (DISCARD)

10 1/2"

12"

4"

4 1/2"

* 4" PVC PIPE

* NOTE: PIPE SIZE IS REFERRED TO BY ITS INSIDE DIAMETER.

84

BASE - MADE FROM 2x3 LUMBER AND 3/4" PLY. WHEELS CUT FROM 2x6 LUMBER.

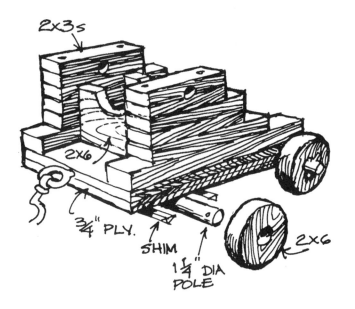

2x3s

2x6

3/4" PLY.

SHIM

1 1/4" DIA POLE

2x6

TO LOAD:
COMPRESS FIRING MECHANISM WITH PLUNGER AND LOCK TRIGGER IN PLACE.

PLUNGER MADE FROM FOAM FISHERMAN FLOATS.

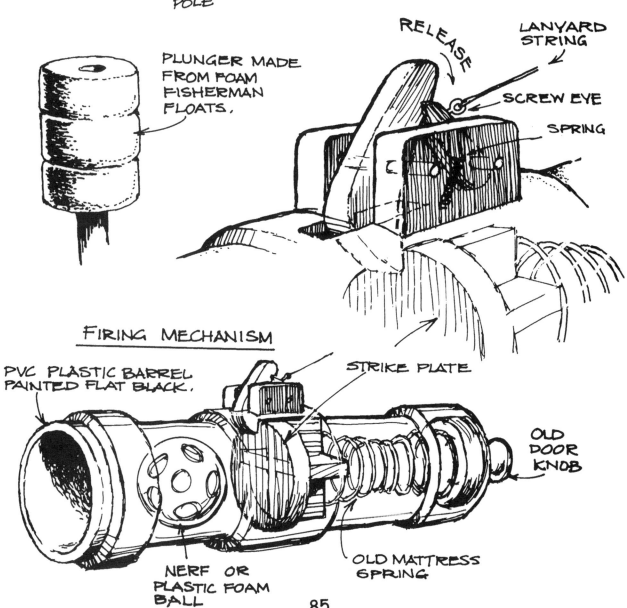

RELEASE

LANYARD STRING

SCREW EYE

SPRING

FIRING MECHANISM

PVC PLASTIC BARREL PAINTED FLAT BLACK.

STRIKE PLATE

OLD DOOR KNOB

NERF OR PLASTIC FOAM BALL

OLD MATTRESS SPRING

SNOW BALL FORT

Snowball forts are made by rolling big balls of snow to one location and piling them on top of one another. If available, place sturdy boards or plywood across the top to provide a roof. Build a wall in front of the fort to act as your first line of defence against an attack. Provide a ledge to hold your snowballs in readiness or build an ammunition sled similar to the one shown on page 96. Make sure you have several holes in the walls to observe "invaders" coming from all directions.

When building a snowball fort, always start with the biggest snowballs on the bottom and add smaller ones on the top. Use loose snow as cement to hold them together.

CITY SNOW FORT

Lucky are you, if you live
in the city during a heavy
snow storm. Wait for the
snow plows to finish clearing
the streets and look for a large pile where they have deposited
their load of snow. Place an old discarded door (the
superintendent in your building might have one) across the top,
shovel out the snow from underneath, and pile it on top of the
door. In fifteen minutes you will have a snow fort.

ASK YOUR SUPT.
TO LOAN YOU A SHOVEL

There is nothing better than waking up to the news that school is "closed due to snow". What a great excuse for parents to play hooky from work -to give their kids a lesson in structural engineering by building a snow fort.

When I think back on my own childhood, the very best time I had with my father was when we built a bigger-than-life size snow sculpture of my pet dog "Skipper". Afterwards, we fooled around throwing snowballs at each other. Every time one of my snowballs hit him he would act as if he was mortally wounded, falling down in the snow moaning and clutching his heart, and I would convulse with laughter.

Snowball Rules

If you make a snow fort, you can assume that sooner or later you will be attacked by your friends. Before engaging the "enemy" make sure everyone knows the rules:

1. Anyone hit three times by a snowball becomes a prisoner of the other side.

2. Prisoners can not be forced to fight against their own side but they can be pressed into service making snowballs for their captors.

3. Anyone throwing an ice ball or a "soaker" or hitting anybody in the head with a snowball will be sent home.

4. Garbage can covers can be used as shields.

TIP: Organize group assault charges accompanied by a great deal of yelling to scare the "enemy" into beating a hasty retreat.

The word "*Igloo*", or "*Iglu*" is purposely omitted here since that is
a general term used by the Eskimos to refer to any kind of house.
This ingenious structure has all the ingredients of a perfect hut.
It cost nothing and takes only three to four hours to build; it
blends in with the surroundings and is warm inside. It is also
strong. Igloos have been known to withstand the weight of a
1000 pound polar bear. Unfortunately it has one drawback - it
melts! A snow house may last only a few days if there is a warm
spell and the temperature goes up above freezing. On the other
hand, it may last all winter, as they often do in Alaska where the
climate is freezing.

How to build an Eskimo snow house the Eskimo way

Materials;

- Rod or cane, 3' long, for testing snow.

- 20 in. knife (Machete)

- Snow shovel for piling snow.

- String, 5' long, with a peg tied to each end for laying out the "footprint" of the house on the snow.

Time: The snow house takes two experienced Eskimos less than three hours to complete.

Procedure:

Find a snowdrift, 4' deep, on level ground away from trees, rocks or snow mounds that may cause snowdrifts later on. Look for snowbanks nearby where you can cut blocks of snow. Test the snow for consistency and texture. If your stick goes through the snow at an even rate (without hitting crusty or soft layers), then the consistency is good.

Step on the snow with a soft boot:

- If you see no impression, then it is too hard.

- If you make a deep impression, then it is too soft.

If you make a faint impression so that a person could just barely follow your trail, then it is just right.

CUTTING THE BLOCKS

BLOCKS ARE CUT INTO A DOMINO SHAPE.

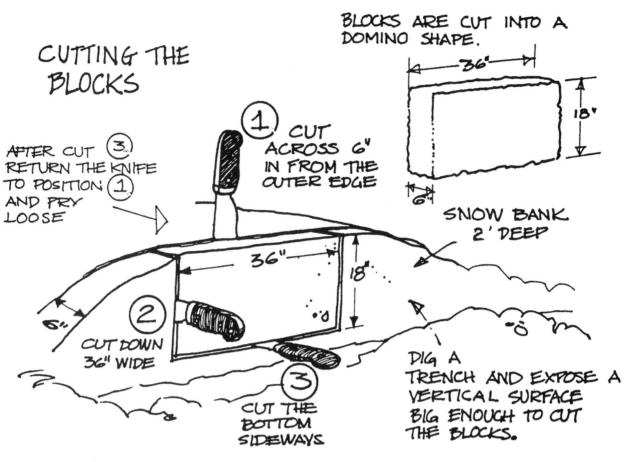

① CUT ACROSS 6" IN FROM THE OUTER EDGE

AFTER CUT ③ RETURN THE KNIFE TO POSITION ① AND PRY LOOSE

② CUT DOWN 36" WIDE

③ CUT THE BOTTOM SIDEWAYS

SNOW BANK 2' DEEP

DIG A TRENCH AND EXPOSE A VERTICAL SURFACE BIG ENOUGH TO CUT THE BLOCKS.

CARRY THE BLOCKS TO YOUR CHOSEN SITE AND STACK THEM IN A CIRCLE READY FOR USE.

MARK A CIRCLE - 10' IN DIAMETER

10 FT. CIRCLE

SHAVE A BIT OFF THE BOTTOM INNER EDGE, SO THE BLOCKS WILL SLANT IN TOWARD THE CENTER AS THEY ARE PLACED ON THE CIRCLE.

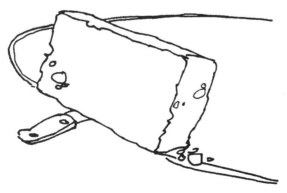

Build the dome by standing inside the walls and having someone hand the blocks over to you.

Start by making a complete circle of blocks slanting inward. If the temperature is right, you will find that the blocks will become frozen together in 5 to 10 minutes.

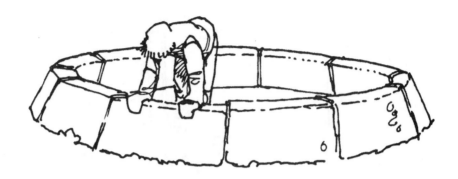

Before you start the second tier, make a diagonal cut slanting upwards and remove the waste.

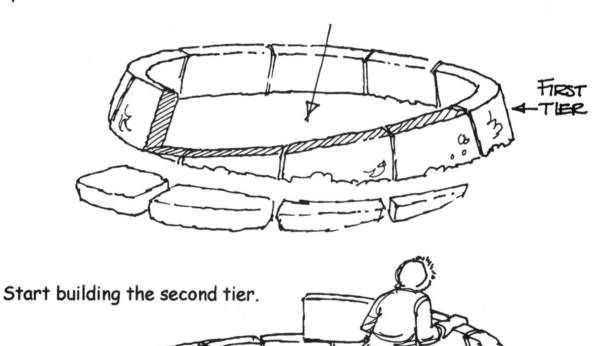

Start building the second tier.

92

Continue to build the wall up in a spiral, always slanting each block in more than the last one so that the structure begins to take on a dome shape.

CUT THE BOTTOM OF EACH BLOCK SO IT WILL SLANT IN.

Once the structure is three tiers high, it may become difficult to have the blocks handed over to you, so cut a hole in the bottom and have them passed through. This hole could later become your door.

Since the blocks are straight and the walls are curved, you will find large crevices at the joints. Gently fill these cracks with soft snow from the outside. This will strengthen the wall.

To fill the remaining hole at the top, select an oversized block, lay it over the hole, and trim it to size with a knife so that it fits like the top of a jack-o-lantern.

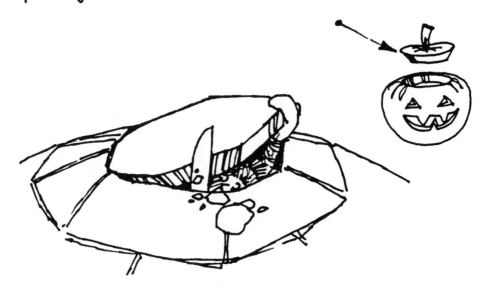

When the dome is finished, shovel loose snow on top and allow it to slide down, filling the remaining cracks and forming a three foot embankment at the bottom.

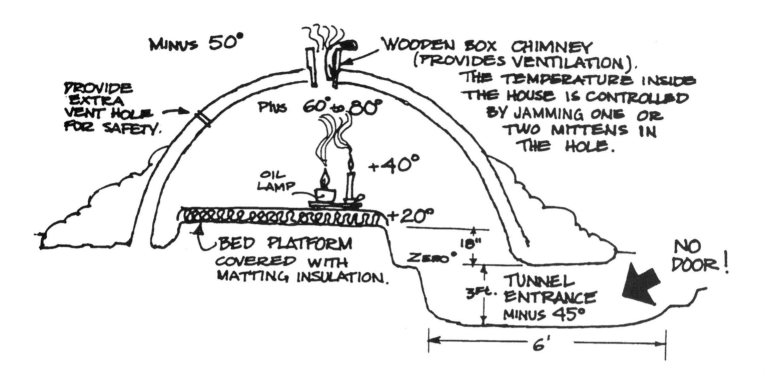

The Eskimo's Secret

The Eskimos found that by digging an entrance tunnel under the house, an air trap occurs making it impossible for cold air to come in at a greater rate than the ventilation hole (chimney) allows it to leave, (see above sketch). Consequently, by burning a small sterno can or seal oil lamp, temperatures of 60 degrees or more can be reached inside when the temperature outside is an unbelievable 50 degrees below freezing. However, it is easier, and a lot safer, to simply cut a hole in the wall, as mentioned earlier.

To increase the strength of the dome, the Eskimos heat its interior to a point where the surface becomes slushy. Then they extinguish the flame and allow the surface to freeze over into ice. This strengthens and insulates the igloo.

One ordinary candle inside the snow house gives off more light than a 50 watt bulb. Because of the nature of the snow, the light inside is diffused and casts very little shadow. Even moonlight is transferred into the interior, illuminating everything in sight.

Although igloos are practically soundproof, a polar bear can be heard several hundred yards away if one has his ear to the floor.

SNOW BLOCK FORT

COMBINATION
SNOW BLOCK MOLD
AND SLED

The "Snow Block Fort" is constructed by first making a plywood box to serve as a mold for the snow blocks. The box is made out of pieces of 3/4" plywood, nailed together, using 1 1/2" finishing nails and varnished to make it slippery.

To build the fort, pack the box with snow and drag it to the fort site. Turn the box upside down and a nice neat block of snow will drop out. Stack up the blocks, as shown above, to make a circular fort.

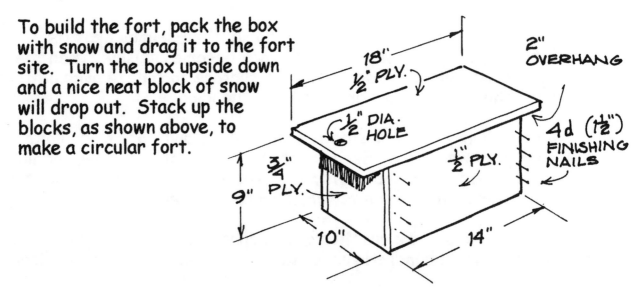

18"
1/2" PLY.
2" OVERHANG
1/2" DIA. HOLE
4d (1 1/2") FINISHING NAILS
3/4" PLY.
1/2" PLY.
9"
10"
14"